FAITH
UNDER FIRE
IN SUDAN

by Peter Hammond

Faith
Under Fire
in Sudan

by Peter Hammond

First published: 1996
Revised and expanded: 1998
Copyright ©1998 by Peter Hammond
ISBN 0-9583864-7-1

Published by:

FRONTLINE FELLOWSHIP
PO Box 74
Newlands 7725
South Africa
Tel: (27-21) 689-4480
Fax: (27-21) 685-5884
E-mail: frontfel@gem.co.za

FOREWORDS

*"How many 'educated' Americans are aware that Sudan is the largest country on the continent of Africa? That, up until the 15th Century, Sudan was a thoroughly Christianized nation before it fell under the influence of Islam? That it is in the grip of the longest war of this century? Or that the most severe persecution of the Church today is to be found in Sudan? Christians everywhere need to be reading **Faith Under Fire in Sudan,** by Peter Hammond. It will mobilize them to support the brave missionary movement of Frontline Fellowship in that suffering part of the world – suffering for the sake of the Gospel of the Lord Jesus Christ."*

– **Dr. D. James Kennedy,** President of Evangelism Explosion International and author of *"What If Jesus Had Never Been Born?"*

*"**Faith Under Fire in Sudan** is the most important and well documented book I have ever read on Sudan, and it encouraged me to pray and work for the Sudanese Christians and for all missions operating in that part of the world. I do believe that no Christian could go to sleep careless after reading this book, be they pastors, politicians, media, businessmen or members of a Christian church. It is a book that cannot be ignored."*

– **Dr. Paul Negrut,** Pastor, Emmanuel Baptist Church, Oradea, Romania.

*"Peter Hammond has been putting his life on the line for nearly two decades advancing God's Word on the frontlines of combat. His book, **Faith Under Fire in Sudan,** gives us facts we need to know and summons us to action."*

– **Howard Phillips,** Chairman of the Conservative Caucus, USA.

"Congratulations on your new book on Sudan! Already God is using it both to raise awareness and to generate prayer."

– **Dr. Tokunboh Adeyemo,** General Secretary of Association of Evangelicals in Africa (AEA)

*"Peter Hammond's **Faith Under Fire in Sudan** is a thrilling account of the power of the Christian Gospel to make Christ's little ones into heroes. Especially Christians in the West need to read this book and to note its message."*

– **Rev. Prof. Dr. Francis Nigel Lee,** Queensland Presbyterian Theological Seminary, Brisbane, Australia

"As the Third Millennium approaches, it is becoming more evident that the centuries-old assault on Christianity by the forces of Islam is heating up. Nowhere is that more evident than in the Sudan where Christians are being murdered, raped, starved and exterminated all in the name of Islam's god Allah. This horror story of the on-going holocaust against Christians in the Sudan is thoroughly and graphically documented in Peter Hammond's new book, Faith Under Fire in Sudan. It is shocking, disturbing, but must reading for all."
– Morgan Norval, Executive Director, Selous Foundation
and author of *"Red Star over Africa"* and *"Death in the Desert"*.

"What a story, what courage to obtain it, what determination it displays about the Sudanese Christians who do not succumb to Islam in its cruellest and worst manifestation in the world today! Would that Christians around the world were to read this sobering account and support our brothers and sisters in the Faith in prayer, publicity and practical help. I have become aware over the past few years of the unpublicised tragedies and astonishing church growth of today's non-Arab Sudan. The world ignores it for the very reason that Frontline's missionaries found - to get the information is both dangerous and costly, and the TV cameramen of today need easier access . . . Faith Under Fire in Sudan is a vital publication . . . It deserves a global distribution."
– Patrick Johnstone, WEC Missionary,
Author of *"Operation World"*

"Faith Under Fire in Sudan is an important document for Christians of all denominations at this time in the history of our continent. We are all aware of the chaos and destruction so rampant on the African continent. What we are not always aware of is the amount of persecution that is taking place on our doorstep against those whose crime is believing in the Lord Jesus Christ. We are also often not aware of the great number of brave missionaries and Christian organisations who are involved amongst these persecuted people as well as in other areas of human devastation where work of relief and compassion is needed. Peter Hammond has done us all a service in focusing our eyes on the Sudan. This long neglected area requires our urgent attention."
– Bishop Frank Retief, Church of England in South Africa,
Author of *"Tragedy to Triumph"*.

Acknowledgements

To compile this handbook on Sudan required painstaking research in the field and a dedicated team. The *Frontline Fellowship* field workers to Sudan: Steve, Derek, Robert, Miriam, Virgil, Elton, Scott, George and Maretha have also had the privilege of ministering in Sudan. Large distances needed to be travelled, many obstacles overcome, delays endured, diseases suffered, dangers risked and innumerable interviews held in order to gather the raw information and photographs for this book.

Similarly I greatly appreciate the outstanding research reports furnished by our friends and colleagues in *Christian Solidarity International* – Gunnar Wiebalck and John Eibner and *Christian Solidarity Worldwide's* Baroness Caroline Cox. Their pioneer work in speaking up for the suffering Christians in Sudan should be an inspiration to all.

For their monumental work in producing the Nuba Mountains Report – *"Facing Genocide: the Nuba of Sudan"* we are grateful to Alex de Waal and Rakiya Omaar, of *African Rights.*

A special word of appreciation is needed for my hosts in Sudan, particularly Rev Kenneth Baringwa, Commissioner Natania Elikimo and Chaplain John.

To Fred Moore for his months of typesetting – especially for putting up with all the last minute alterations and additions – a very special thank you!

To Miriam Cain and Robert Zins for helping with the proof reading and to Julie Valentine and Charles Boyle for the cover design, artwork and layout. I am very grateful.

May the Lord abundantly bless each of you for your investment in this project. May this book be used for the glory of the Lord and may Sudan be blessed with faith and freedom, life and liberty, peace with justice.

DEDICATION

To my parents-in-law, **Rev Bill** and **Harriett Bathman,** missionary pioneers who fear God, love liberty and have devoted 38 years to serving the persecuted churches throughout Eastern Europe. Their lifelong dedication, vision and love for their suffering neighbours continues to inspire me and countless other Christians worldwide.

Thank you for entrusting your missionary daughter into my care. Although we work on different continents we share the same burden and mission to suffering Christians. May God grant that your grandchildren grow up to love, worship, honour, serve and obey our Lord Jesus Christ more faithfully and effectively than we have done.

FAITH UNDER FIRE in Sudan

Contents

		Page
	Glossary and List of Abbreviations	1
	Chronology	2
	Map	4
1.	A Country of Contrasts	5
2.	An Overview of Sudan in History	9
3.	Gordon Pasha and the Mahdi	13
4.	Sudan in the Bible	29
5.	The Growth of the Church in Sudan	31
6.	Jihad and Genocide	36
7.	The Forgotten Frontline	40
8.	Fighting for Survival	51
9.	In the Sudd	60
10.	Slavery in Sudan	70
11.	War Intensifies in Southern Sudan	75
12.	Genocide in the Nuba Mountains	83
13.	The Quranic Connection	93
14.	Corruption and Deception – The UN in Sudan	96
15.	Overcoming Obstacles to Sudan	100
16.	Love in Action at the Battlefront	112
17.	Serving the Suffering in Sudan	130
18.	Strafed and Bombed in the Nuba Mountains	142
19.	SPLA Offensive Overwhelms Muslim Forces	146
20.	The Victory of the Cross	151
21.	The Gospel versus Jihad in Sudan	159
22.	The Liberation of Western Equatoria	172
23.	Why did Christianity Die Out in Northern Sudan?	176
24.	Jihad – Islamic Holy War	180
25.	Under Siege in the Nuba Mountains	189
26.	Speaking Up for Sudan	209
	Appendix: Messages from Sudan	212
	Linguistic and supplementary maps	217
	Organisations involved in Sudan	220
	Sudan at a Glance	221
	Bibliography	222

GLOSSARY AND LIST OF ABBREVIATIONS

ACROSS	Association of Christian Resource Organisations Serving Sudan
Anyanya	Term popularly used for the resistance fighters in the first war (1955-1972)
Dar el Salaam	So called peace camp or concentration camp
FF	Frontline Fellowship
GOS	Goverment of Sudan
Jebel	Arabic word for mountain
Jihad	The Sixth Pillar of Islam - "Holy War"
ICRC	International Committee of the Red Cross
Khalwa	Koranic school
Kujui	Arabic word for traditional priest
LS	Sudanese Pound (at time of writing LS1500 = US $1)
NGO's	Non-Governmental Organisations
NIF	National Islamic Front
Mahdi	A military messiah selected by Allah for Holy War
OLS	Operation Lifeline Sudan
PDF	Popular Defence Force
RCC	Revolutionary Command Council
Shari'a	Islamic Law
SSIM	South Sudan Independence Movement
SPLA	Sudan People's Liberation Army
SRRA	Sudan Relief and Rehabilitation Association
UN	United Nations Organisation

CHRONOLOGY
Some key dates in the history of Sudan

712 BC The Cushites under Piankhi conquer Egypt establishing the 25th dynasty.

671 BC Cushites pushed out of Egypt by invading Assyrians.

23 BC Roman invasion of Nubia, capital Napata sacked and most of Nubia annexed to the Roman Empire.

37 AD Conversion to Christ of the treasurer of Queen Candace - the Gospel first comes to the Kingdom of Meroe (present day Northern Sudan).

250 AD Persecution under Decius.

297 AD Persecution under Diocletian

297 AD Roman withdrawal from Sudan.

350 AD Invasion of Meroe (Sudan) by the Christian Axumite Kingdom of Ethiopia.

580 AD Christianity becomes the official religion of the kingdoms of Nubia.

643 AD Islamic military invasion repulsed.

652 AD Second Muslim military expedition defeated.

1484 More from internal decay than from outward attack Christianity died out in the Northern Sudanese Kingdom of Dotawo after the death of the Christian King Joel.

1530 The fall of the Christian Kingdom of Alwa heralded the demise of Christain faith in the North of Sudan.

1821 Invasion of Sudan by Ottoman ruler of Egypt. Escalation of slave trade.

1873 General Charles Gordon, appointed Governor in Southern Sudan, launches a vigorous campaign to eradicate the Islamic slave trade.

1881 Widespread rebellion under Mohammed Ahmad (who declares himself the *"Mahdi"*) erupts.

1885 Khartoum is captured and after a courageous stand General Gordon is killed attempting to defend Khartoum from the Mahdi's forces.

1898	The forces of the Mahdi are defeated at the battle of Omdurman by the British Army.
1956	Civil war erupts between the Muslim North and the Black South as Independence is declared.
1956	Sudan votes in a plebiscite (referendum) against union with Egypt.
1958	Incensed by the government's failure to subjugate the South, General Ibrahim Abboud leads a military coup which overthrows the government.
1964	Following the military regime's failure to defeat the South, the October Revolution overthrows the military regime and elects Sadiq al-Mahdi (the great grandson of the Mahdi) as prime minister.
1969	Colonel Jafaar Nimeiri leads another military coup which overthrows the government.
1972	The Addis Ababa Agreement suspended the North-South war by granting the South a measure of autonomy and religious freedom.
1983	Following the abject economic failure of Nimeiri's socialist schemes, *Shari'a* (Islamic law) is declared. This abrogation of the Addis Ababa Agreement sparks a renewed civil war.
1985	A popular revolt overthrows the military regime.
1986	The first elections in 20 years result in the return of the former prime minister Sadiq al-Mahdi who had been deposed in 1969.
1989	A military coup by Lt. Gen. Omar Hassan Ahmed al-Bashir overthrows al-Mahdi and institutes an extremely militant Islamicist regime under the National Islamic Front. War intensifies.

SUDAN

- - - International boundary
- - - Regional boundary
——— Road
- - - - Track
——— Railroad
⊙ National capital
◉ Regional capital
○ Town, village
✈ Airport

The boundaries and names shown on this map do not imply
official endorsement or acceptance by the United Nations.

MAP NO. 3814 UNITED NATIONS
MARCH 1994

1

A COUNTRY OF CONTRASTS

Sudan is the largest country in Africa. It is also the most difficult to travel across. It is a country of contrasts stretching from the equatorial rainforests and swamps of the Sudd in the South, through the Nuba, Jebel Marra and Red Sea mountain ranges to the Sahara Desert in the North. Even today a large section of this vast country remains to be explored. It is one of the world's last frontiers.

Sudan takes up 8% of the African continent and 2% of the world's land surface. It is about one-third of the size of the USA. There are only 30 million people in this vast area, but they constitute over 140 ethnic groups and speak 117 languages. Here too the contrasts are great – between the Muslim Arabs of the North (70% of the population), and the Christian Blacks (20%) and Animists (10%) of the South. Arabic is the official language of the Muslim North and English has been chosen as the official language of the rebel controlled South!

Sudan is only for the hardiest and most adventurous travellers. It is as hot as a furnace from March to September, and the rainy season transforms the roads and tracks (where they exist) into thick streams of mud. The only kind of vehicle that can survive the harsh terrain is a four wheel drive. Driving in some parts of Sudan is extremely tough on both the vehicles and their occupants. One Frontline Fellowship mission team took 12 hrs to drive just 180 km. On one of my trips it took us 8 hours to drive 120 km. On another stretch of road two very determined motorcyclists took 3 hrs to cover just 2 km in loose sand! The unbearable heat often persuades travellers to do their driving at night. Temperatures of 48°C (118°F) or more are not unusual in the North. Even in the "cooler" South, temperatures of 37°C (98°F) with humidity at 80% or more are common. By way of contrast it can be bitterly cold at night, particularly in the desert areas where it can even reach freezing point!

The South is covered by savannah, elephant grass, swamps and forests. Elephants, buffaloes, lions, cheetahs, leopards, giraffes, zebra, hippopotamuses, antelope, chimpanzees, baboons and crocodiles are present in fair numbers. Snakes, scorpions and tsetse flies are also quite common. The heat in the South is so intense that the White Nile loses about 60% of its water in evaporation as it passes through the Sudd. The Sudd is an area the size of Pennsylvania which is transformed into a swamp during the rainy season.

International human rights and relief agencies rate Sudan as amongst the five countries in the world with the worst score on the *"human suffering index"*. In terms of the availability of clean drinking water, daily calorie intakes, education, political freedom, civil rights and life expectancy, Sudan rates as having the highest level of suffering and the lowest level of freedom in the world.

The Sudanese are some of the very poorest people on earth. Yet they are also some of the most generous and hospitable. Strangers are welcomed into homes for tea, food, fellowship and a place to stay overnight. Even on buses, trains, ferries and camel caravans, Sudanese people will usually share whatever food or drink they may have with those around them.

Potentially, Sudan is a wealthy country. The Red Sea Hills have substantial mineral deposits and oil reserves have been identified in the South West and North West of Sudan. With Africa's largest river, the Nile, flowing through it, Sudan has immense agricultural and pastoral potential. Yet the scorched earth policies of the Islamic government have devastated the South. What was once called the *"Breadbasket of North Africa"* has become the site of the worst man-made famine in the world. About two million people have died since 1983 as a result of either the war or the famine. Five million more people have lost their homes and are internal refugees.

The war continues to cost the Khartoum government US $2 million a day. The national debt of the government of Sudan is over US $16 billion (50% more than the Gross Domestic Product). Sudan cannot even pay the interest on its debts. Imports outweigh exports by about 20 to 1.

Unemployment is very high. The average annual income per worker is US $390 (2% of USA average). Inflation has averaged 150% to 200% per year. The price of bread rose 500% in one year.

Despite having the greatest concentration of medical needs on the continent, the shortage of doctors is severe. Malaria, tuberculosis, meningitis, hepatitis, trachoma, bilharzia and dysentery are common. Yet there are only about 4 000 doctors (one for every 6 500 people) in Sudan according to official statistics. However, these medical practitioners are concentrated in and around Khartoum. In the South there is one doctor for every 83 000 people. Several medical relief workers have been killed in the war (mostly executed by government militia, for providing first aid to wounded rebels). This has hardly encouraged the relief agencies nor has it stimulated the tourist industry. What it has helped to stimulate is emigration. Over 70% of the country's trained doctors and surgeons have left the country.

Aside from famine, disease, persecution and war, Western Sudan is plagued by bandits who are not inclined to stop at robbing their victims. Torture and murder are their specialities. The *National Islamic Front* police and security forces are little better. The arrival of foreigners is often seen as a rare opportunity to (slowly) flex the muscles of their bureaucratic obstructionism and to test their (considerable) harassment skills.

Yet while Sudan is the site of the most vicious anti-Christian persecution raging anywhere in the world today - the Church is growing faster in Sudan than anywhere else I know of. It would appear that more Muslims are coming to Christ in Sudan than anywhere else in the world. Twenty years ago the Christians made up 5% of the total population. Today Christians comprise over 20% of Sudan (and 80% of Southern Sudan). Sudan is a land of extremes and contrasts.

Popular Defence Force soldiers are taught to use guns at a training camp near Khartoum. Students must undergo military training. Volunteers are sent to the war in the south (Abbas/Magnum).

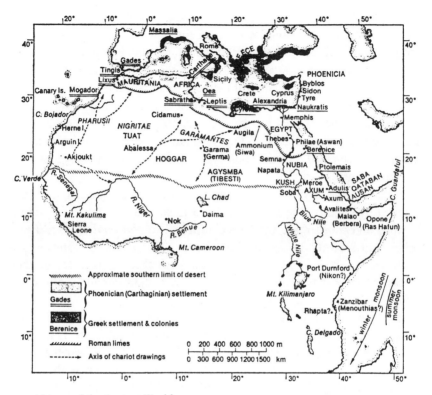

Africa and the Ancient World.

2

AN OVERVIEW OF SUDAN IN HISTORY

To the Egyptians, Sudan was known as the land of Cush: the source of ivory, incense, ebony, gold and slaves. Sudan was subjected to numerous Egyptian trading and raiding forays until the 8th century BC. Then Cush grew to be a great power and under their King Piankhi the Cushites conquered Egypt in 712BC. The Assyrians later invaded and seized Egypt from Cushite control in 671BC.

The influences of Egypt, Greece, Rome and India are evident in the temples, tombs and pyramids built in Northern Sudan. The cursive Meroetic script of the Cushite kingdom still remains undeciphered and so most of its history remains mysterious.

In 23BC an invasion force of Romans - 800 cavalry and 10 000 infantry - swept into Sudan, sacked the capital Napata and annexed a large part of Nubia. The Romans withdrew in 297AD. Then the Christian Axumite kingdom of Ethiopia invaded and ensured the fall of the ailing Meroe kingdom. Over the next centuries the three kingdoms of Northern Sudan were converted to Christianity. Their united efforts blunted the first wave of Muslim invaders in the 7th century. Subsequent Islamic efforts to conquer or convert the Nubian Christian kingdoms failed.

It was only in the 13th century that internal Christian squabbling and massive Arab immigration brought about the demise of Christianity and the rise of Islam in Northern Sudan. The Ottoman Turkish influence increased from the 16th century on.

At the beginning of the 19th century the Ottoman ruler of Egypt, Mohammed Ali, launched a series of attacks on Sudan. Mohammed Ali was a ruthless and power hungry army officer who had gained control of Egypt with the help of the Mamluks, a mercenary military class who were originally Turkish slaves. Later when the Mamluk leaders posed a threat to Mohammed's power he eliminated them all by massacring them at a banquet he had called in their honour.

Mohammed's 25 year old son, Ismail, was sent off with 10 000 men to raid Sudan. Ismail's troops were promised 50 cents for every human ear they brought back. 3 000 ears and 30 000 slaves were sent back to Cairo on the first caravan (although only half of the slaves survived the journey). The Sudanese then counter-attacked and Ismail died a fiery death in his own tent. Mohammed retaliated with more invasions and by 1823 over 50 000 Sudanese had been killed and Sudan was firmly under Egyptian control.

With the building of the Suez canal and Egyptian bankruptcy, Britain became the dominant power in both Egypt and Sudan. In 1873 the Christian General, Charles Gordon, was appointed governor - first of Equatoria province, then in 1877 of all of Sudan. General Gordon's campaign to stamp out the Islamic slave trade created a crisis. The Muslim community was enraged and declared that *"the supression of slavery was against the principles and traditions of Islam"*. Open rebellion erupted.

A local Muslim leader, Mohammed Ahmad, declared himself *"Mahdi"* (a military messiah selected by Allah to lead a *"Jihad"* or holy war). The *Mahdiyya Movement* which resulted has continued to influence Islamic politics in Sudan to this day. The *Mahdi* besieged Kordofan and starved the inhabitants into submission. His forces then rampaged throughout Sudan. General Gordon made a courageous stand against all odds in Khartoum which ultimately fell in 1885. The forces of the *Mahdi* were finally destroyed at the battle of Omdurman in 1898 and Sudan entered an almost 60 year period of peace where slavery was effectively suppressed.

Along with independence in 1956, Sudan erupted into civil war - between the Arab North and the Black South. Military coups in the Muslim North in 1958 and 1969 only intensified the war. Then in 1972 the Addis Ababa Agreement temporarily ended the war by granting the South autonomy and religious freedom.

This uneasy peace was shattered in September 1983 with the dictator Col. Nimeiri's declaration of *"Sharia"* (Islamic law). Khartoum's liquor stocks were thrown into the Nile causing considerable pollution and the inebriation of many fish.

*Sudan's military leader
Lieutenant-General Omar Hassan
Ahmad al-Bashir, (AFP)*

*Sheik Hassan al - Turabi secretary
of the National Islamic Front is
believed to wield the real power
in Sudan.*

*SSIM is led by Dr Rick Machar
Teny-Dhurgon (Peter Moszynski).*

*Dr John Garang de Mabior is the
leader of SPLA-Mainstream (Panos).*

John Garang (a graduate of Iowa State University) and a member of the Dinka tribe, then reactivated the *Sudanese People's Liberation Army* (SPLA). Within 2 years the SPLA had 25 000 armed soldiers under it's command. Their spectacular victories led to the Muslim military coups in 1985 and 1989, when the successive disgraced dictators were replaced by other frustrated Muslim leaders. By 1989 over 90% of Southern Sudan had been liberated by the SPLA rebels.

In the early 1990's however, the rebel's position was substantially weakened by tribal infighting. The Muslim dictator Lt. Gen. Omar Al-Bashir of the *National Islamic Front (NIF)* then took advantage of these divisions by launching a series of dry season offensives from 1992 onward.

These offensives have gained temporary ground (mainly towns) which inevitably are cut off and besieged by the rebels during the rainy season.

South Sudan remains as the oldest Christian community in Africa, a bulwark against the Southward advance of radical Islam. It is on the very frontline of the fight for faith and freedom.

SPLA soldiers of the 7th Division in training with captured G3 rifles.

3

GORDON PASHA AND THE MAHDI

The most extra-ordinary example of the clash of cultures and religions in Sudan came about in the latter half of the 19th Century. The legacy of the English Christian General Charles Gordon (or Gordon Pasha as he is remembered) and of the Arab Muslim *Mahdi* Mohammed Ahmed ibn Abdullah continue to influence Sudan to this day.

Charles Gordon, whose life and death was destined to have such a great impact upon the history of Sudan, was born in England in 1833, the fourth son of a Royal Artillery officer who rose to be a lieutenant-general. Charles was described as a resourceful and aggressive youngster with a keen eye and fiery temper for injustice. At 16 he entered the Military Academy and at 19 began his training for the Royal Engineers - an elite professional corps in the 19th Century. It was the engineers who carried out reconnaissance work, led storming parties, demolished obstacles in assaults, carried out rearguard actions in retreats and other hazardous tasks.

Gordon first saw action in the Crimean War in southern Russia where he gained a reputation for fearlessly scouting enemy positions under fire in the front line - always returning with accurate field sketches and useful intelligence.

Gordon was critical of the general lack of offensive spirit and was disgusted by those whose zeal was less than his. He wrote of the *"indescribable"* excitement of war and how he enjoyed it *"amazingly"*! He was mentioned in Despatches and after the war was appointed assistant commissioner to an international commission to survey the new Russian-Turkish boundary. For three years this preoccupied him in Bessarabia and Armenia.

Thereafter Captain Gordon was sent to China where he reconnoitred 400 miles of the Great Wall. He also began a charitable fund for paupers, contracted smallpox and began to seriously consider *"eternal things"*. At about this time Tien Wang (or the *"Heavenly King"* as he called himself) inaugurated a new *"Dynasty of Perpetual Peace"* by starting a vicious civil war. Hundreds of thousands died at the hands of these Taiping rebels - many by being beheaded, crucified or buried alive. Yet these so called *"freedom fighters"* received widespread support from British liberals with some missionaries writing ecstatic accounts of sober, God-fearing *Wangs* (the title given to Taiping rebel leaders)!

In 1863 Major Gordon was appointed as Commander of a Chinese mercenary force which had been optimistically named the *"Ever Victorious Army"* (EVA)! He took to this task of suppressing the extra-ordinarily successful Taiping Rebels with ingenuity. He turned the enemy's two greatest assets to his own advantage. Because the Taipings were better fighters than his own Chinese troops he spared prisoners' lives and enlisted captured Taiping into his EVA. The many intricate waterways which serve as obstacles to advances, Gordon turned into routes for supply and attack. He utilised a large flotilla of small ships to transport his artillery and infantry down the canals to outflank the Taipings and bring his guns to bear.

Gordon conceived it to be the duty of a commanding officer to personally lead critical assaults. This he did with calm courage and competence. In 16 months he planned and executed 16 major offensives capturing or destroying most of the Taipings and their weaponry. Amidst the battles he rescued many an orphan. At the height of the Quinsan battle he was seen carrying a naked urchin who, educated at his protector's expense, grew up to be a senior police officer in Shanghai.

Gordon succeeded in defeating the rebellion by aggressive leadership and indirect tactics - with little loss to his own forces. He earned the reputation of being extra-ordinarily tough, working day and night, a man of courage, resolution and, when necessary, ruthlessness. He ended up as a Marshall in the Imperial Chinese Army but refused literally a roomful of gold as reward. In fact he refused any payments beyond his regular British Army pay. He returned in 1865 to England as a celebrity - lionised by the press as *"Chinese Gordon"*.

His father's death in the year of his return to England revived his spiritual interests. It was from 1865 that he dated his true conversion to Christ. Before this he wrote that *he: "had a belief that Jesus was the Son of God and used to have feelings of deep depression on account of my faults".* Now *"I know Jesus is my Saviour. God made me count the cost and conclude that His service should be all . . . the fruits of the Spirit could be had only by abiding in Christ . . ."*

Gordon gave himself wholeheartedly to Christian service in his community: visiting poor families, sick people and lonely people whom he befriended. For the rest of his life he was involved in the relief of the sick, the suffering, the poor and particularly the homeless orphans. His family mansion became a mission house. He ran a free school from his home where, every evening, he taught reading, writing, arithmetic and history. There was also cricket, chess and cheerful hymns. The "scuttlers" from the slums normally arrived filthy and were washed by Colonel Gordon. Planting the freshly cleaned and clothed boy in front of a mirror Gordon would say: *"Just as you see a new boy on the outside, I want you to be new inside as well!"* Gordon gave them a home, food, clothes, teaching and a knowledge of God and His Word. He also helped to find them employment.

After eight years of such inner city missionary activity in England Gordon was invited to replace Samuel Baker as governor of Equatoria (the Southernmost province of Sudan). His mission would be to establish order and suppress the slave trade in over 200 000 square miles of thorn shrub and swamp. Like the Moses who despised the riches of Egypt Gordon refused the £10 000 a year which the Khedive of Egypt offered him. Gordon accepted the governorship for only £2 000 thus contributing to the growing belief that *"Chinese Gordon"* was not quite sane.

Sudan at that time was a colony of Egypt which in turn owed allegiance to the Turkish Empire. The Khedive Ismail (an Albanian Muslim) who ruled Egypt was himself a slave owner on a gigantic scale - as were most of his relatives, friends and ministers of state. But as this was bad for his image in Europe - from where most of his investments came - Ismail instructed Gordon to stop the slave trade in Sudan. Thus the Khedive could continue to enjoy the services of innumerable slaves in Egypt and at the same time earn the reputation of an enlightened leader opposed to slavery!

As governor of Equatoria, Gordon soon learned that almost all of his Egyptian soldiers had been sent to Sudan as a punishment. Stunningly unmotivated, these ill-clothed, ill-fed, unpaid conscripts were

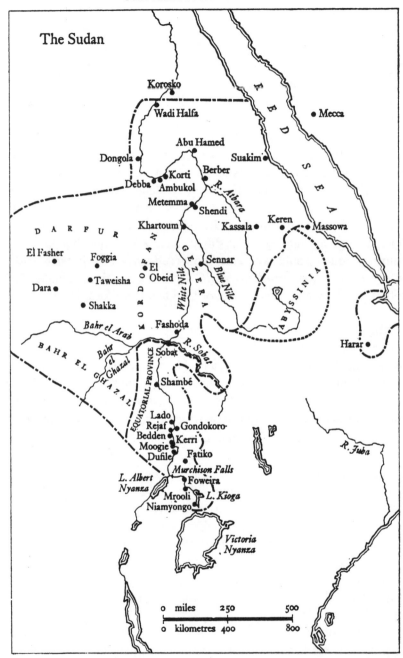

The Sudan

Korosko

Wadi Halfa

Mecca

Abu Hamed

Dongola

Suakim

Korti

Berber

Debba

Ambukol

R. Atbara

Metemma

Shendi

D A R F U R

Khartoum

Kassala

Keren

Massowa

El Fasher

Foggia

El
Obeid

Sennar

Dara

Taweisha

White Nile

Blue Nile

A B Y S S I N I A

Shakka

K O R D O F A N

G E Z E R A

Bahr el Arab

Fashoda

Harar

Bahr
el
Ghazal

R. Sobat

B A H R   E L   G H A Z A L

EQUATORIAL PROVINCE

Sobat

Shambé

Lado

R. Juba

Rejaf

Gondokoro

Bedden

Kerri

Moogie

Fatiko

Dufile

Murchison Falls

L. Albert
Nyanza

Foweira

Mrooli

L. Kioga

Niamyongo

Victoria
Nyanza

| o | miles | 250 | | 500 |
| o | kilometres | 400 | | 800 |

Sudan in Gordon's time, 1870's.

16

never allowed leave lest they desert. Yet with such unpromising troops Gordon would suppress the slave trade, explore the Great Lakes and introduce law and order to Equatoria!

The possession of slaves in Sudan was legal. It was the traffic in slaves that Gordon had to suppress. Slavery was easy money. Adventurers could obtain loans, boats and slave raiders in Khartoum, sail up the Nile river and, in partnership with some co-operative chief, the slavers would raid a few villages at dawn. A few would be shot or speared, the rest captured. The elders would be tortured to reveal their hidden ivory.

Adults were secured with a *sheizba* (a heavy forked pole) resting on the shoulders, the head secured by a cross-bar, hands tied to the pole. Of the survivors who reached Khartoum, females were allocated to concubines or domestic service. Most of the males became labourers or servants. The lucky ones became *Bazingers* (slave soldiers) to carry out slave raids on others. The unlucky males were castrated for household service (this operation, performed in unsanitary conditions - without anaesthetics - was often fatal).

By-products of the slave trade were cattle and ivory captured or bartered, which were carried by the slaves. The average slaver could aim on capturing 400 to 500 slaves (worth £5 or £6 each) and 20 000 lbs of ivory (worth £4 000 in Khartoum) a year. The thriving, stinking, fly-swarming city of Khartoum prospered on the twin trades of slaves and ivory.

There was hardly an official in Sudan who was not involved in these trades. It would have been hard to find a household in Khartoum so poor as to not own at least one slave. Even the most pious and humane Muslims were unable to see why the Christians made such a fuss about slavery. *"It might be wrong to enslave Muslims"* went their argument, *"but the economics of Sudan required a constant flow of fresh slaves and the vast majority of these were pagan blacks. Could any reasonable man deny that the life of a Negro - as a slave in Egypt, Turkey or Syria - was infinitely preferable to his life in Equatoria or the Congo where life was poor, nasty, brutish and short!"* So went the common rationalisations in defence of the Islamic slave trade.

It was estimated that seven-eights of the population of Sudan were slaves!

Gordon's first action against the slave trade was to nationalise the ivory trade – which denied slavers much of their profit. Then he closed the Nile river to slavers. This unfortunately had the unforeseen result of immeasurably increasing the sufferings of the slaves. Instead of being crammed like sardines into boats down the Nile the slaves were now marched across the pitiless desert!

Gordon improved communications down the Nile, multiplied military outposts throughout Equatoria and set about introducing the rule of law. It was a very personal administration. Justice was swft. Criminals were flogged. It was effective. It was popular with the people. However, it only worked because of Gordon's impartiality. With anyone less fair and conscientious it would have doubtless been abused. Gordon's was the first example of a foreign rule which could be fair, conscientious and incorruptible.

At Rejal over 100 armed men of the Niam Niam tribe, who were reportedly occasional cannibals, surrounded Gordon and after drumming all night advanced threateningly on him. Gordon drew two guns and ordered them: *"Now, go!"* They went and left him alone. On another occasion a mob of hostile Bari men threatened Gordon. As the witch-doctors seemed to be performing some cursing ceremony on him, Gordon fired a shot into the ground beside them. This ended the ceremony and the threat.

Gradually movement became easier in Equatoria. The people began to see that they could receive justice even against the Governor's own servants. When Gordon began his work in Equatoria its only exports were ivory and slaves. Slavers operated with impunity. A healthy young woman could be purchased from her parents for a packet of needles. By the time Gordon left, a respect for human life had once again returned to Equatoria.

As the slave routes had now moved across the desert to Bahr-el-Ghazal, Gordon wrote to the Khedive requesting the position of Governor-General of the whole of Sudan. This was granted.

Gordon's Sudan was 1 640 miles long and about 660 miles wide. His first task as Governor General was to see the whole Sudan – and to be seen by it. Within five months Gordon rode over 5 000 miles by camel across the scorching desert sand, stony steppes, wooded uplands and steamy swamps. He used thoroughbred racing camels capable of long journeys at an average of 7 miles an hour. He owned a team of 5 camels so as not to wear them out and he read books while riding at a trot. The desert strengthened the tendencies towards asceticism and mysticism already strong within him. As others before him had been prepared for their life work in the desert, so too Gordon became even more spiritually attuned.

Gordon enjoyed the drama of swooping down like an avenging angel upon a lethargic garrison of a remote desert outpost, leaning forward in the high saddle, legs pressing on the camel's shoulders – as he was depicted in the famous statue later erected in Khartoum. During this camel tour of Sudan, Gordon suppressed a revolt, and the robber chieftains of Bahr-el-Ghazal cowered into submission. He neutralised the largest and most dangerous slave trader, Suleiman Zebeyr, disbanded half his slave army and took the rest into his army – all without firing a shot.

Gordon succeeded in breaking the back of the slave trade in Sudan with prayer, pressure, persuasion and his overwhelming personality. These experiences convinced him that there were no limits to what he could achieve by audacity and faith in God.

In one of his writings, Gordon rebuked Christians for lacking in self denial and devotion. *"A man must give up everything, understand everything, for Christ."*

Gordon was ruthless with incompetent officials. He sacked many lethargic and corrupt officials and created momentous upheavals and disruptions in the administration. When he investigated the prisons he found them to be dens of injustice with many prisoners detained for years without trial. Gordon somehow found the time to look into every case. Corruption, false testimony and incompetence had led to many miscarriages of justice which he endeavoured to reverse. He summarily had a notorious murderer hung and the city was quieter for it. He had a man hanged for castrating a slave. Many unjustly detained without trial were released.

In just two months Gordon captured 12 slave caravans. One of these, after crossing 500 miles of desert, had only 90 out of the original 400 slaves surviving. Few were over 16 years, some of the girls had babies and there were many small children.

He caught many of his own officials and soldiers involved in the slave trade. Gordon ordered that the governor of any district through which a captured slave-train was proved to have passed should forfeit 3 months pay. When a Royal Navy vessel captured a large slave ship off-shore of Massawa, Gordon solemnly handed over 3 months of his own salary.

SLAVERY·

At Shaka he expelled 100 slave dealers, 4 who were proven guilty of a massacre were shot. Fourteen slaves were rescued from a small party of 3 slavers whom Gordon had flogged and dismissed. To tighten the blockade of Bahr-el-Ghazal, Gordon authorised the Baggara tribe to arrest slavers.

Financial problems in Cairo precipitated a change in government. The ousted Khedive Ismail was replaced by Khedive Tewik, a Turk. This led to Gordon being replaced as Governor General of Sudan. Yet Gordon left behind a transformed Sudan. He had abolished the *Courbach* (whipping the soles of the feet for not paying one's taxes), stamped out corruption, freed many who had been unjustly imprisoned and freed many slaves. He had also remitted back taxes and provided piped water for Khartoum.

He was popular in Equatoria as the man who had, at least temporarily, freed them from the Muslim North. However he was resented, though respected, by the Arab North. His prestige was higher than his popularity. Most Sudanese value the courage of a warrior very highly and Gordon's courage was unquestioned. They may have resented having a Christian govern them but they respected his piety and devotion. They may have deplored his attacks on the slave trade but they also appreciated his zeal, energy and integrity. Gordon was admired more for who he was than for what he had done.

While Gordon was leaving Sudan, another leader was living as a hermit on the island of Aba, 200 miles up the White Nile from Khartoum. In May 1881, at the age of thirty-eight, Mohammad Ahmed ibn Abdullah proclaimed himself the *Mahdi*. This was after years spent in prayer, fasting, Quranic study and contemplation of the decay of Islam.

The Sufi sect which predominated in Sudan widely believed in the coming of the *Mahdi* (the Expected One - an eschatological figure whose advent foreshadowed the end of the world). The Sufi leaders and teachers known as *fakis* and their dervish disciples widely believed that in the year 1300 of the *Hegira* (1882 of the Christian Calendar) the *Mahdi* would reveal himself. They were therefore predisposed to accept the claims of Mohammed Ahmed who was a member of the Sammani order of Sufis. He came from the west of the Muslim world, not as had been predicted from the East, but otherwise he was everything the *Mahdi* should be: devout, learned, descended from the Prophet and he carried the sign of a

Mohammed Ahmed ibn Abdullah (The Mahdi).

mole on his right cheek. There had been others claiming to be the *Mahdi*, but none came as close as he did to matching the prophecy.

As the successor of the Prophet, the *Mahdi* claimed temporal authority over all Muslims and spiritual authority to restore the purity of Islam. He had chosen an opportune time to announce his uprising. There was widespread resentment of Turkish (foreign) rule and many thousands had been bankrupted by the suppression of the slave trade. The *fakis* and dervishes responded to his religious appeal, the riverine tribes desired the return of the lucrative slave trade and the Baggara nomads were basically against any government (which meant taxes). When the *Mahdi* forbade the paying of taxes to Khartoum and announced a return to the slave trade his popularity was assured.

Imitating Mohammed, the Mahdi made his Hegira retreat to the Jebel Quadir in the Nuba Mountains of Kordofan. The Baggara joined him by the thousands. Three punitive expeditions against the Mahdists were annihilated and the rebellion flourished.

Meanwhile there had been a military coup in Cairo. And a massacre of Christians in Alexandria led to a British Naval bombardment and an expedition under (Gordon's lifelong military friend) General Wolseley to protect the Khedive against his army and foreigners against the mob. On 13 September 1882, Wolseley routed the Egyptian army at Tel-el-Kebir. This began Britain's occupation of Egypt - which although it was meant to be brief lasted for 70 years.

During this time Gordon was promoted to Major-General and appointed Commandant General of the forces in the Cape Colony in South Africa. Gordon soon made his strong and unpopular opinions known. The Boers who had recently thrashed the British Army at Majuba were men after his own heart - brave, frugal and pious. As for the natives - they had been badly treated and promises made to them had been broken.

Gordon visited the exiled Zulu king, Cetshwayo, in Cape Town and spoke with him of spiritual matters. Neither did Gordon neglect the spiritual welfare of the Boers. He had one of his tracts translated into Dutch and distributed quantities around the countryside for the God-fearing burghers to study. Gordon's prime responsibility was to settle the Basuto border question. During this time he had dealings with Cecil Rhodes who found him an extra-ordinary man - one who was disinterested in money! Finally Gordon resigned complaining that it was *"not possible to do anything with such a weak, vacillating government"* as that in Cape Town.

Gordon then took long leave and fulfilled his cherished ambition to spend a year of research in the Holy Land. He declared it to be the happiest year of his life - a routine of prayer, Bible study and examining Jerusalem and other historic sites where Jesus had ministered. He set out to resolve through investigation the site of the crucifixion, the place of the Holy Sepulchre (the empty tomb) and other Biblical issues. His book *"Reflections in Palestine"* was, to him, his most prized achievement.

On 8 September 1883 a British Colonel Hicks, in command of an Egyptian force of 10 000 unmotivated soldiers, marched into Kordofan in search of the *Mahdi*. On 5 December his rabble was annihilated along with himself and all his officers. This military disaster placed Khartoum itself at risk.

As Britain was occupying Egypt, it was now also responsible for Sudan. However, after Britain's humiliating defeats at the hands of the Zulus at Isandlwana (1879) and by the Boers at Majuba (1881) the liberal government wanted to get out of Egypt and stay out of Sudan.

Unwilling to send an army to relieve Khartoum, the prime minister, Gladstone, agreed to send General Gordon. A total of 21 000 Egyptian and Sudanese soldiers scattered throughout Sudan were confronted by 300 000 dervish (Mahdist) rebels armed with modern rifles and artillery captured from Hicks.

Without a British army it seemed impossible that Gordon could put down such a vastly superior force as that led by the Mahdi. Yet General Gordon felt duty bound to rally to the support of Sudan in its time of crisis.

Appointed Governor General of Sudan and ordered to evacuate all foreigners, Gordon arrived to an enthusiastic welcome in Khartoum. He immediately halved taxes and abolished tax arrears making a huge bonfire of tax records. He also announced the independence of Sudan from Egypt, appointing a council to rule under himself as Commissioner of Her Majesty's Government. He then sought to have Britain declare Sudan it's protectorate. Being surrounded by the Mahdi's forces he reported that an evacuation was impossible and requested a relief column.

Once their land routes were cut off and even the telegraph was cut, Gordon ceased being a politician and concentrated on being a soldier. He brought immense reserves of courage, determination, and invention into improving the defences of Khartoum. Whilst negotiating with the Mahdi by letter, he strengthened the fortifications of Khartoum with a ditch, rampart, land mines and wire entanglements. He also abolished customs duties and the pass system at the gates of Khartoum. This was to encourage villagers to bring more produce into the market, which they did.

Gordon converted the steamships into armoured warships with cannons. These steamers were used for sorties to break up enemy concentrations, for raids to capture cattle and excursions to buy grain. Gordon's defence was active, imaginative and aggressive. Gordon himself engaged in sharpshooting to take out enemy snipers. As the siege tightened artillery duels were fought.

During all this time a groundswell of public outrage was brewing in Britain. Newspaper editorials denounced the government's indecisiveness, evasiveness and dishonesty. *The Times* called for prayers for *"General*

Gordon's last stand in Khartoum as depicted in this Victorian painting.

Gordon in imminent peril at Khartoum". Even Queen Victoria added her voice to the public demand for the British government to send a relief column. The outcry was perhaps motivated by humanitarian concern, commercial interests, admiration for Gordon's courage and dedication to duty, hatred of the slave trade, national pride offended by being defeated by the dervishes and even evangelical missionary fervour. Finally, the British government felt compelled to send a relief column under General Wolseley - but under serious restrictions which unnecessarily delayed their progress.

Incredibly several hundred of the Mahdi's soldiers deserted and came over to join Gordon's starving besieged garrison! The British relief column smashed the Mahdi's force of 10 000 dervishes at Abu Klea on 17 January 1885 causing much fear in the *Mahdi's* camp.

Just after midnight on 26 January 1885 over 60 000 dervishes attacked Khartoum - swarming across the defences, overwhelming the thin line of weakened troops. The Mahdists poured into Khartoum slaughtering both soldiers and unarmed civilians indiscriminantly.

There are two main accounts of Gordon's death. The first account to reach Cairo - by one who never claimed to be an eyewitness - had Gordon, calmly and unresisting, being speared to death. As this was the first version to be published and as it has been immortalised in a famous painting it has been generally accepted. However, two key eye-witness accounts - one by a bodyguard of Gordon and the other by a dervish warrior - agree that Gordon went down fighting: As the Mahdists broke into the palace garden Gordon stopped them in their tracks with revolver fire from upstairs. He then rushed to a wounded man's aid and was hit in the shoulder by a spear. The enemy came on again. He fired again until he ran out of ammunition and then lunged at them with his sword. A dervish shot him in the chest knocking him back against a wall. He recovered again and with his sword beat back the enemy down the stairs. At this point he was felled with a spear thrust in his right side.

The reader may take his choice. The unresisting Gordon may accord with contemporary pacifist notions of a martyr, but all his life Gordon had been a fighter - the weight of evidence is that he died not like a lamb but like a lion.

Two days later the British relief column arrived. The British public reacted with rage. The Queen sent a furious telegram to her prime minister. Briefly it was considered whether to press on and re-establish British prestige, but Gladstone's liberal views and innate pacifism reasserted itself. All British troops were withdrawn from Sudan.

Six months after Gordon's death, the *Mahdi* died. A succession of poor harvests, epidemics and tribal wars reduced Sudan to misery. An attempted invasion of Egypt by the Madhists in 1891 was soundly defeated.

In due course, with a Conservative government in power in England, the time was chosen to avenge Gordon. Under General Kitchener a vast Anglo-Egyptian army advanced up the Nile and crushed the Mahdist army outside Omdurman. Sudan was then ruled as an Anglo-Egyptian condominium. On the whole it was the most successful and altruistic of all Britain's colonial ventures, from which Britain gained very little and from which the Sudanese people benefited a great deal. Nowhere was the departure of the colonial power regretted more deeply than in Gordon's Equatoria.

When, after independence, the statue of General Gordon was overturned there was a howl of protest from the older residents of Khartoum: *"He was a man of God."*

As with any great man, Gordon has received some vicious criticism from detractors who hate what he stood for and choose to assail his character. Some have depicted him as a drunkard, yet no one ever saw him drunk. He did drink (yet never in the field or *"on safari"* as he put it), but was reportedly never immoderate in his consumption of alcohol. He also gave up alcohol regularly. It is extremely improbable that he could have been a habitual drinker. At the cracking pace he worked, with as little sleep as he had, in the harsh climates he travelled and with as many enemies as he had - neither his health, nor his work nor his reputation in the Sudan could have endured it.

Others have attempted to portray him as a homosexual. This completely unsubstantiated slander is part of the homosexual community's strategy of claiming as many respected figures of the past as their own in order to gain some respectability by way of association. The fact that Gordon never married and that he devoted much of his time to rescuing orphaned boys from the streets is hardly evidence of homosexuality, yet on this basis there has been much speculation. Yet, Gordon was a strict Victorian Christian gentleman who wrote scathingly against *"the effeminate"*. He was appalled by the *"reprehensible"* *"sin of Sodom and Gomorrah"*. Again with all the many enemies he had it is remarkable that not once in his 51 years did anyone of his contemporaries suggest the slightest bit of scandal - aside from his disdain for money!

One criticism, which is true, is that Gordon had a fiery temper. He did not tolerate incompetence, indolence or dishonesty. He was a tiresome perfectionist. Yet as he was quick to wound so he was quick to apologise. He never lost his power to compel love, fear and obedience from those around him. He had his faults, yet there is no doubt that he was a devout and sincere Christian, a courageous soldier and a compassionate leader who cared for the poor and the helpless. His legacy is still seen in Equatoria where Christian soldiers strive to follow his courageous example by fighting for faith and freedom. There he is affectionately remembered as Gordon Pasha.

Gen. Charles Gordon first as Governor of Southern Sudan, later of all Sudan, effectively eradicated the slave trade. After leading a courageous stand against the Muslim Mahdi, General Gordon was killed and beheaded in Khartoum.

4

SUDAN IN THE BIBLE

"Cush will submit herself to God."   **Psalm 68:31**

In the Bible, Sudan is also referred to as Cush, Nubia and Ethiopia. Often when the Bible mentions a place at the end of the world it would refer to Sudan. *(e.g.: Ps 87:4).*

Moses' second wife was from Cush *(Numbers 12:1).*

2 Kings 19:1-9 and *Isaiah 37:1-10* relate how one of the Cushite Pharaohs, Tirhakah, intervened in Israel to assist King Hezekiah when he was attacked by Sennacherib, the emperor of Assyria.

The prophecy in *Isaiah 18* could well refer to Southern Sudan. It speaks of a land *"beyond the rivers of Ethiopia"* which worships the Lord God. They are described as *"a nation tall and smooth of skin,"* feared all over the world. The prophecy declares that there will be great bloodshed there and a spiritual revival. Some people believe it refers to the Zulus or the Afrikaners in South Africa, while others believe it accurately describes Southern Sudan.

In *Zephaniah 3:10* a similar prophecy is given: *"From beyond the rivers of Ethiopia My worshipers, the daughters of My dispersed ones, shall bring My offering."*

Nahum 3:9 describes how the Assyrians treated the Egyptian city of Thebes when the Cushites were defeated.

Jer 38:7-13 describes how a Sudanese official, Eben-Malech, helped save Jeremiah from certain death in a dungeon.

Acts 8:26-40 relates how the evangelist Phillip explained *Isaiah 53* to an Ethiopian official, the treasurer, from the court of Queen Candace. The Sudanese kingdom of Cush ruled from Meroe from about 350BC to about 350AD. The conversion of the Ethiopian treasurer from the Kingdom of Meroe in 37 AD marked the beginning of the Church in Sudan.

Early Christian murals at Faras Cathedral in Nubia. The large winged figure is the Archangel Gabriel who is shown protecting Shadrach and his campanions in the fiery furnace (Daniel 3). (Circa AD 1050).

The rare and beautiful stained glass Communion Chalice discovered in a hiding place under the High Altar at Faras Cathedral. This was probably a gift from the Empress Theodora of Byzantium (Circa AD 600).

5

THE GROWTH OF THE CHURCH IN SUDAN

The first Sudanese to be converted to Christ was the treasurer of Queen Candace in AD37. *(Acts 8:26-40)*

During the 3rd Century many Egyptian Christians fled to Sudan during the persecutions of the Roman emperors Decius (250AD) and Diocletain (297AD). A strong Christian community was flourishing in Philae from at least 350AD. Crosses and other Christian objects have been found in the royal tombs of Nubia dating back to the 5th Century.

Following the collapse of the Kingdom of Meroe (in about 350AD) three smaller Kingdoms were established - Nubia, Makuria and Alwa. The middle kingdom of Makuria was converted after the missionary work of Julian. One early writer described the conversion of the Nubian king, Bahriya, as the key event: *"When Bahriya was converted to the religion of Christ, all the Blacks of Nubia followed him, and he built for them churches throughout the land of Nubia and many monasteries which are still flourishing."*

By 580AD Christianity had become the official religion of the kingdom of Nubia. Many thousands became monks. Archaeologists have unearthed over a hundred churches dating back to this period in Nubia. Many of these churches have elaborate paintings on the walls.

After the death of Mohammed in 632AD the peaceful growth of the Churches in the Nile valley was shattered. Arab armies rapidly spread out throughout the Middle East. Egypt was conquered in 642AD. The Islamic armies then launched an attack on Nubia in 643AD. The Nubians steadfastly resisted and threw back the invaders. Again in 652AD a Muslim military expedition sought to conquer Nubia. Again they were defeated by the Nubians. After their military failures the Muslims entered into an agreement called the *Baqt* which established peaceful relations and trade between Muslim Egypt and Christian Nubia. The peace lasted almost 600 years until about 1250AD.

From 900 to 1200AD Nubia enjoyed a golden age of peace, prosperity and Church growth. One of the popular hymns still sung today was composed at that time:

> *"The Cross is the hope of the Christians;*
> *The Cross is the resurrection of the dead;*
> *The Cross is the path of them who wandered;*
> *The Cross is the guidance of the blind;*
> *The Cross is the staff of the lame;*
> *The Cross is the nurse of the suckling;*
> *The Cross is what strengthens the feeble;*
> *The Cross is the physician of the sick;*
> *The Cross is the perfection of the priests."*

In 1172AD the Fatimid rulers in Egypt (who upheld the *Baqt* agreement) were overthrown by Saladin. Then in 1260 another revolution in Egypt brought the Mamluks to power. The Mamluks then waged a series of wars against the Nubians. Towns were burnt and confusion spread. Gradually the weakened kingdom fell into chaos and into the control of the Mamluks. The kingdom of Dotawo started to break up over the next 150 years. The last Christian king, Joel, fell in 1484.

The southernmost Christian kingdom of Alwa survived successive attacks in the 14th and 15th centuries. In 1450 a missionary to Ethiopia wrote this about Nubia: *"The people are neither Christians, Muslims or Jews, but they live in the desire of being Christians."* The recorded history indicates that very few Nubians converted to Islam. Christianity began to die out because of internal weaknesses in the Churches and **not** because of the external attacks of Islam.

The missionary Avares wrote of Sudanese who came to Ethiopia from Alwa: *"While we were in (Ethiopia) there came six men from (Alwa) as Ambassadors to the King, begging him to send them ministers and monks to teach them. He did not choose to send them."* This was the last we heard of the Church in Northern Sudan. An island of Christianity in a sea of Islam, isolated and cut off - they appealed to their Christian neighbours in Ethiopia. Tragically, this help was refused.

Eucharist Service at an Episcopal Church Conference in Moruland.

Youth Choir of a Nuer Presbyterian Church in Upper Nile.

By the 1600's word reached Rome of groups of Christians surviving South of the Sahara. The pope set up the *"Mission of Upper Egypt-Funji-Ethiopia"* and several missions (in 1698, 1705 and 1711) were sent up the Nile to make contact with the believers. The final attempt in 1794 ended with Father Ballerini being murdered in Nubia. From 1849 the Catholics established a string of mission stations - in Khartoum, Yondokoro, Kanisa, Kakor and elsewhere. Forty-six missionaries died of disease in the first few years. In 1862 alone, 22 missionaries died. Finally all the mission stations were abandoned and the survivors returned to Europe.

A new Catholic attempt to reach Sudan was launched in 1873 with schools and farms as the priority. This strategy succeeded and today almost half of those who claim to be Christians in Sudan are Catholics.

In 1885 after the fall of Khartoum and the beheading of Gen Gordon, the Church Missionary Society raised funds for a mission to Sudan in honour of General Gordon's pioneer work and witness. They were followed by the United Presbyterian Church of America and later the Sudan Interior Mission and Africa Inland Mission. Hospitals and schools became the focal points of the new Protestant missions.

Revivals broke out in Yambio and Moru County in 1938. Bible translations into Bari, Zande, Moru, Acholi, Dinka and Nuer continued from the 1930's to the 1970's and to this day. So far, 8 languages have full Bibles, 17 have only New Testaments and 12 have only portions of the Bible translated. Translators are still working on 22 languages.

In 1957 the Muslim government seized control of all the mission schools. In 1960 Sunday was replaced by Friday as the day of rest. Those who protested were imprisoned for years. *Khalwas* (Islamic schools) were built throughout the South. Their ruins are still a reminder of how much they were resented. In 1962 *The Missionary Societies Act* attempted to restrict missionary work by forbidding evangelism of those under 18 years old. In 1964 all missionaries were expelled and persecution intensified.

Yet the Church has increased tenfold over the last 30 years. Today the steadfast and resilient Christian Church in Sudan is one of the fastest growing in the world.

SPLA soldiers celebrate a recent victory with songs of praise.

Bible distribution in Equatoria.

6

JIHAD AND GENOCIDE

One of the greatest tragedies in Africa is Sudan. Sudan, the largest country in Africa, is engaged in the longest war in African history. One of the oldest Christian nations in the world, the Nubians have been severely persecuted by the Muslims from the North for centuries.

From 1899 to 1955 Sudan experienced, for the first time in many centuries, peace and efficient, honest administration led by a few hundred dedicated British and Egyptian expatriates. At insignificant cost, successful economic schemes were launched transforming desert scrub into productive cotton fields.

However, since independence in 1956 more than half the land once under cultivation reverted to scrub and there are now 5 million peasants herded into refugee camps. Millions more have been slaughtered in the Islamic Jihad or have succumbed to starvation and disease.

Since 1956 the successive Muslim governments of Sudan have waged a series of vicious wars against the non-Muslim Black population in the South. The UN estimated that in 1993 alone excess ("abnormal") deaths due to the war in South Sudan amounted to 220 000.

Since 1983 the Government of Sudan (GOS) army and militia have subjected the Nuba Mountains area to a scorched earth campaign. The Muslim military units have looted or destroyed civilian grain supplies and cattle, bombed their villages, enslaved large numbers of people and engaged in arbitrary detention, torture and summary executions of Christians and Animist Blacks. Approximately 70% of Sudan's 27 million population are Muslims, 10% are Animist and 20% are Christians.

A crowd of 2 000 Muslim women demonstrated in Khartoum on 8 September 1993 protesting against the United States (Associated Press).

A vicious war between the Muslim Arab North and the Christian and Animist Black South raged from 1955 to 1972. The 1972 Peace Agreement provided for a degree of autonomy for the South and recognition of their religious convictions. However, when Sudan was declared an Islamic Republic in 1983 and Islamic law was enforced upon the Christians in the South, the war erupted again. The entrenchment of even more extreme Islamicists in Khartoum in 1991, led to an intensification of the already severe conflict. Sudan has become a base for Iranian revolutionaries to spread their brand of Islam by terrorism. In 1993 Sudan was placed on the US State Department's list of terrorist states. Sudan's leaders proudly boast that they are the leaders of the Islamic Revolution in Africa.

Tragically the cost of this Islamic Revolution for Sudan has so far been a devastated economy, a divided country and the deaths of approximately two million people.

One Christian Solidarity International (CSI) fact-finding mission to Sudan reported: *"Christian believers are denied freedom of worship and are Islamised by force. Government of Sudan troops are burning churches and killing Christian leaders."* They witnessed the aerial bombardment of villages by Sudanese government forces and saw the mass starvation caused by the Muslim scorched earth campaign.

They received sworn testimonies from eyewitnesses who had survived massacres, crucifixions, the burning of churches and crops, and enslavement. They documented cases of Muslims literally crucifying Christians and enslaving their children.

The CSI report concludes: *"Our inescapable conclusion is that the Government of Sudan is systematically destroying the fabric of society in the South and the Nuba Mountains by means of terror and hunger. In short, the Government of Sudan is committing genocide."*

As one Sudanese Christian summed up their plight: *"We are committed to Christianity and that is why we are suffering."* Bishop Gassis of Sudan issued this message: *"The silence of the leaders in Europe, USA and Canada and their procrastination - tomorrow and tomorrow - is helping the Government of Sudan to eliminate its people through genocide and ethnic cleansing. The indifference and silence of Christian leaders is condoning the inhuman acts being perpetrated by the regime. Their silence is killing our people."*

This man received 20 lashes from a police officer immediately after he was arrested for drinking alcohol by a Public Order Court (Abbas/Magnum).

Prisoners sentenced to death in civilian courts are liable to be hanged. Other methods of execution include stoning to death, crucifixion and execution by firing squad (Mark Stucci).

Beaten to death: Christian being killed by a Muslim mob in Sudan (Photo from Voice of the Martyrs).

7

THE FORGOTTEN FRONTLINE

Christians are literally fighting for their lives and liberty in Sudan. The Christians in South Sudan have stood firm as a bulwark against the expansion of militant Islam into Central Africa for 14 centuries!

The vast Sahara desert is a barrier that separates the Arab Muslims of the North from the predominately Christian Black South. Sudan stands at the crossroads of Islam and Christianity in East Africa. The great Nile river has historically served as a channel for the expansion of Islam into the heart of Africa. For centuries the Black nations south of the Nuba mountains have courageously and effectively resisted every attempt by the North at Arabization and Islamization.

The relentless waves of cruel Islamic slave raiders during the 19th Century only deepened the resolve of the South Sudanese in their complete rejection of Islam. The vicious civil war between the Muslim Arab North and the Christian Black South since 1955 has even further entrenched the Christians' determination to defend their faith and freedom from Islamic aggression. Yet, despite this being the longest war in the largest country in Africa, few Christians seem to be aware of the extraordinary sufferings and heroism of our Sudanese brothers and sisters in Christ.

It was just before dawn, in December 1993, when the Muslim army attacked Sadagh village. The soldiers had left their vehicles and had approached the village on foot. Suddenly they opened fire with rifles, RPG rockets and grenades. There was no resistance from the local population who fled. The Muslims then burned the church and school and most of the homes. The mosque, however, was left untouched. They also looted all the cattle, goats and sheep. Two young Christian girls were captured and taken into slavery.

The Muslim Militia, the *Popular Defence Force* (PDF), sell young Black children to be slaves to Muslim masters for between $35 and $95. These slaves are usually dressed in just one piece of cloth, a red *jallabia,*

Sudanese soldiers and civilians stand in front of Kober Prison in Khartoum. Hundreds of political prisoners have been held in Kober Prison since the al-Bashir government seized power on 30 June 1989 (Popperfoto).

Most political detainees are held in harsh conditions in so-called "ghost houses" run by the security services. (Amnesty International)

Criminal prisoners in leg-irons in Kober Prison 1994. (Amnesty International)

to be easily recognised if they attempt to escape. The boys are usually used to tend the cattle of the Bagarra and Rizeigat tribes whose youth have been conscripted into the Muslim army or militia.

Escape From Slavery

A Dinka tribesman testified how his ten-year-old daughter and eight-year-old son had been taken from him in Aiel in 1992 by the Muslims. After many weeks he and his wife managed to find the slave camp where his children were being indoctrinated in Islam. He described it as a large camp with many straw buildings each occupied by 50 to 60 children. Most of these children were from Nuba or Dinka tribes.

The children were forced to attend the Islamization school and to cultivate the large *durra* farms around the camp. By God's grace he and his wife managed to locate their children, sneak out of the camp and escape back to their village with their children.

Michael was an eleven-year-old boy who was rounded up with other Christians in the market place by the Muslim police. The boys were interned in a camp where they lived under armed guard and were subjected to severe beatings with camel whips. All the boys were from Dinka, Nuer and Nuba tribes. They were all given Islamic names and not permitted to use their Christian names or ancestral family names. Michael was renamed Mohammed. They were forced to learn how to pray and recite Koranic verses in Arabic. Failure to perform led to savage beatings.

When Michael and his three friends tried to escape they were caught and flogged. They were then forced to hold a brick in each hand above their heads for a long time. After another failed escape attempt and more severe punishment, Michael and his friends, managed to escape and return to their families.

The majority of Sudanese women also suffer systematic discrimination, repression and degradation at the hands of the *National Islamic Front* (NIF). Women have often been arrested and flogged for failing to adhere to Islamic dress codes. One Christian lady reported that she was arrested and flogged for failing to adhere to Islamic dress codes.

Another Christian lady reported that she was arrested and threatened with sexual abuse for not wearing an Islamic veil.

> *"The Chief officer . . . wanted me to pay the cost of releasing me - in bed! Of course, I refused . . . In court I saw many women and the police were hitting them. I fell to the ground and fainted."*

Once she recovered the judge sentenced her to be lashed. This was carried out immediately in front of the judge. *"They took the shirt off my back and then lashed me. When I kept silent and was not affected, the judge said I defied him and ordered them to lash me in excess."* These floggings are normally done with a camel whip and they leave deep and permanent welts on the skin.

Human Rights Watch Africa reports that in Sudan, under Islamic law, the testimony of a woman is half that of a man. Marriage contracts and *hudud* offences are heavily biased against women. Many of the women prisoners reportedly sleep in the open courtyards of the overcrowded prisons.

The Cross Under the Crescent

Restrictions on Christian churches date back to the *Foreign Missionary Society Act of 1962* which treats churches as foreign rather than domestic entities and forbids the building of churches without strict government control and permission. Routinely such church applications have been refused. Many hundreds of churches have in fact been burned to the ground with many pastors and elders crucified. All missionaries were expelled from the South of Sudan in 1964.

Children are not admitted to primary education in Sudan unless they have received two years of Koranic instruction in a Muslim *Khalwa*. Adherence to Islam is also a condition for admission to university. Access to the war and famine stricken areas has been denied to non-Muslim aid agencies. Food aid is being withheld from non-Muslims. Christians have been forced to move to Muslim controlled areas to survive. They are then urged to renounce their faith and beg *"in the name of Allah"* to receive food aid.

Women in the Popular Defence Force militia training at Khartoum airport (Abbas/Magnum).

Thousands of Nuba have been killed and tens of thousands of others cleared from their villages by force and settled in government-controlled "peace villages" (Peter Moszynski).

Hundreds of Christians are routinely arrested - without warrant - in arbitrary swoops. These believers are then held in detention, without any charges being laid against them and without any opportunity to communicate with their families. Torture is routinely used in interrogations. Merely partaking in communion wine during a church service has been sufficient cause for a sentence of 40 lashes to be imposed on a Christian.

Survivors of the infamous *ghost houses* of Khartoum, El Obeid and Port Sudan report enduring the following torture tactics: immersion of their heads in water until they suffocated, burning with cigarette ends, electric shocks, mock executions, the pulling out of finger nails, rapes and other degrading and cruel punishments.

Nor have such abuses been limited to Christians. Muslims who have fallen foul of the fanatical NIF elite have received even worse tortures. For example Brig Mohammed Ahmed al-Rayah al Faki (age 53) presented the following sworn testimony:

> *"I was tried by a secret and summary military tribunal (23/3/91) one month after my arrest . . . During the 18 months I spent in Shalla I suffered: severe beatings with a water-hose and whipping on the head and all over the body, chaining and suspensions, locked in suffocating containers, sexually abused with solid articles, my sexual organs were crushed by pliers, electric shocks . . ."*

Dr Sharif, the chief surgeon at Port Sudan Hospital, issued a medical certificate supporting the Brigadier's testimony: *" . . . he suffers from a slipped disc and testicular atrophy . . ."*

Abd al-Bagi al Raya, a lawyer in Khartoum had to have his leg amputated after 48 days of torture. Another lawyer had a plastic bag with hot pepper placed over his head, was whipped, beaten and underwent repeated mock executions. He witnessed 380 executions of fellow Muslims (mostly from the *Sudan National Party)* just because they failed to fully support the extreme NIF Islamization policy.

Public debate in Sudan has been silenced. All political parties have been banned. The Supreme Court has even upheld the right to extract confessions under torture, and crucifixion as a form of execution, as being compatible with Islamic *Shari'a* law and the Penal Code of Sudan!

In accordance with the NIF's social engineering plans, the homes of hundreds of thousands of people have been bulldozed down or razed to the ground. In 1991 the authorities relocated over 150 000 "displaced persons" and "squatters" from the capital city, Khartoum. During 1992 the authorities forced an additional hundred thousand people to an inhospitable terrain far outside the city. Many of the homes were destroyed to discourage any attempt to return. Fifteen people who resisted this move were killed.

Medicines Sans Frontiers (MSF) calculated that over 100 000 more people were forcibly relocated from Khartoum between November 1993 and June 1994, and a further 60 000 in July 1994. Most of these displacements took place in night time raids with the razing of entire townships. These newly displaced people are now too far from Khartoum to commute to work from there and the opportunities for employment near these resettlement camps are minimal.

Meanwhile the offensive to subjugate the South Sudanese Christians continues. The Nuba Timu tribe near Lagawa has almost been eliminated. According to *Human Rights Watch Africa*, all the male population that failed to flee to the mountains have been massacred. The eldest males in the villages are 7 years old. Almost all the females from 14 years and up are pregnant. Most of the population now live in the so called *"Peace Camps"* where *Khalwas* (Islamic schools) have been erected.

Refugees from Gogrial, Aiel and Mayom spoke of widespread famine as a result of the Arab scorched earth policy. Crops were burned, wells were poisoned and livestock were looted. The *Mujahidin* and PDF took advantage of a cease fire agreement with the SPLA to attack many unprotected Christian villages and make off with their cattle. In Gogrial a plague had broken out - devastating the survivors.

Yet, amidst these tragedies, the strong faith and courage of the Sudanese Christians has been forged. One pastor of a village which had endured aerial bombing and military occupation by the Muslims declared:

> *"Though we are hungry, thirsty and dying of disease, we will take up our cross to show the world that we are Christians."* Then he asked: *"So why doesn't the Christian community in the rest of the world raise its voice on our behalf?"*

46

*An air raid drill at Palatako school. Civilian targets
been regularly bombed by the Government of
Sudan Air Force.*

Despite the relentless persecution, the churches in Southern Sudan are experiencing phenomenal growth. Twenty years ago only 5% of Sudan claimed to be Christians. Now 20% identify themselves as Christians. In the South of Sudan 80% of the population attend Christian services. One denomination has grown from 2 to 140 congregations in just 10 years.

For many, becoming a Christian is an expression of opposition to Islam - so nominalism is still a problem. However, for many their conversions are a genuine work of the Holy Spirit. Revivals have broken out amongst the Nuer (Presbyterian), Dinka (Episcopal), Mabaan and Uduk (Sudan Interior Church), Acholi (Africa Inland Church) and some of the Nuba tribes (Sudanese Church of Christ).

The persecution has been particularly severe in the Nuba Mountains where the Muslims have declared a *jihad* (Holy War) against the (Arabic speaking) Nuba peoples. Like the Armenian Christians in Nagorno Karabakh, many of the Nuba peoples are an island of Christianity in a sea of Muslims - cut off from the larger body of Christians in the South. The policy of the Khartoum government is to eliminate the Nuba people by the destruction of their villages, the massacre of their men and enslavement of their women and children.

Faith and Freedom

In the face of this *jihad* many Christians in the South have taken up arms under the banner of the *Sudanese Peoples Liberation Army* (SPLA). There were two major factions of this movement. One under Commander John Garang is fighting for the total independence of South Sudan. The other faction under Dr Riak Machar claimed to be fighting for autonomy for the South in a unified Sudan. In effect the SSIM under Machak seemed to spend far more time fighting the SPLA than the Muslim government.

The SPLA resistance fighters have inflicted some serious defeats upon the Muslim *Mujahidin* and PDF militia. Major victories have been achieved near Lagawa, Juba and Way. Muslim military convoys have been ambushed and valuable munitions captured. Entire divisions of the Sudan army have been wiped out in offensive actions by the SPLA. Most of the Equatorial and Upper Nile provinces are securely in SPLA hands.

For most boys, army life begins as soon as they are old enough to handle a rifle - normally 14 or 15, sometimes at 12 or 13 years old.

Life in Sudan is very primitive. There are virtually no cars, no machines, no electricity, no medicines. Just about the only signs of technology are the AK47 Kalishnikov assault rifles, Makarov pistols and RPG rocket launchers.

The climate is oppressively hot - with walls of fine dust blowing across the dry sun-scorched land. The heat is relentless and the sound of buzzing flies, mosquitoes and other flying insects is continuous. Most of the people are shockingly malnourished. Many seem to be living skeletons with leathery skin stretched over their bare bones. Heat, dust, flies and starvation are ever present companions and the sound of gunfire is seldom far away.

This is the forgotten frontline of the fight for faith and freedom.

Peter ministering with an SPLA unit in Western Equatoria.

SPLA soldiers load an anti-aircraft gun in Southern Sudan as government bombing of villages intensifies.

8

FIGHTING FOR SURVIVAL

"The Muslims cannot defeat us. We stand firm as Christians, and we will die for our faith. Our struggle is not against Islam or against Muslims, but is against a regime that wants to destroy our African heritage and faith. It is discouraging to see that the Islamic dictatorship in Khartoum receives material and moral support from other Islamic countries, while we receive no support from the Christian world. But we will continue our struggle for freedom even if we are forsaken by Christendom. We will die for our faith and we will die as Christians."

These are the words of Commander Thomas Cirillo of the *Sudanese Peoples Liberation Army* (SPLA) as he led the siege of Kapoeta. Cdr Cirillo had served as an officer in the artillery corps of the Muslim army of Sudan until July 1993. After he was converted, he convinced his troops to join him in a mutiny. They changed sides and joined the Christian forces - the SPLA.

The Muslim government *Popular Defence Force* (PDF) had captured Kapoeta in May 1992. Immediately the new commissioner, Abdalla Kapello, began to enforce the Islamisation and Arabisation policies of the government of Sudan. A Koranic school was established. Christians who defied his orders by continuing to worship in churches were arrested and beaten.

The head Sunday School teacher, Pio Napomba, was arrested and taken to a *"ghost house"* where he was tortured. At one point his captors tied a sack filled with red pepper around his head. This practice often leads to an agonising death by asphyxiation. Pio, however, survived and was later released. Meanwhile his son, Stephen, and assistant, Philip, were arrested for conducting Bible studies. When the Muslims offered them freedom in return for admitting their guilt and promising not to proclaim the Gospel - they refused. Stephen and Philip were then subjected to the red pepper torture. Later Stephen and Philip escaped to the SPLA lines outside Kapoeta.

By this time all the civilians had been evicted and 2 000 Muslim soldiers had turned Kapoeta into their barracks. Cdr Cirillo tightened the siege around Kapoeta and began to bombard the Muslim forces. Despite repeated air attacks by government Antonov bombers, the SPLA forces still had the government troops trapped in their underground bunkers according to the last report. A relief column was allowed into Kapoeta only to swell the numbers of those trapped.

Cdr Cirillo reported that the Muslim mujahadeen and militia customarily chant before battle: *"We will force you to become Muslims whether you want to or not."* He claimed that the government forces kill all SPLA soldiers who fall into their hands, while the SPLA routinely take prisoners and treat them according to the Geneva Convention. A local minister confirmed that the Commander had about 200 Muslim prisoners of war and that he was able to regularly visit and minister to them. The pastor was satisfied that they had been treated humanely.

During the siege, the church building in Kapoeta was occupied, fortified, mined and desecrated by Mujahadeen volunteers and members of the PDF. A Muslim soldier was shot by the SPLA as he attempted to cut down the cross on the roof of the church. PDF troops were driven out of the church compound during a fierce battle on November 10, 1994. Bishop Taban intended to resume church services in Kapoeta once the area was secured and the church compound had been cleared of mines. However, during a subsequent offensive the Muslims again siezed Kapoeta.

Testimonies Amidst Tribulation

Clement Deng was born into an Animist Dinka family. When he was 12 years old, he left home to serve a Muslim family. At this point Clement was persuaded to become a Muslim and enrolled in a Koranic school. He was troubled, however, by the way the teachers justified the killing of all Christians and other non-Muslims who refused to recite the Islamic creed. After much heart-searching, Clement became a Christian in 1977.

Clement's conversion infuriated his fellow students in the Koranic school. When he was warned that he had been condemned to death (the penalty prescribed by Islamic law for *"apostasy"*) and that his former friends now planned to kill him, Clement fled to Wad Medani. There he served in the local church until the war erupted in 1983.

A local Arab Muslim leader, Abdullahi, was converted to Christ after he saw a vision of the Lord Jesus. He managed to persuade his whole clan to be converted to Christ and this provoked the Muslim authorities into a violent rage. Amidst the ensuing persecution, Clement fled to Khartoum. While he was serving in the church in Arkwet (a suburb of Khartoum), Clement came to know some Christian boys who had been captured in the South and interned in an

SPLA soldier and boy.

Islamic slave training camp. These boys were soon to be sold as slaves to Saudi Arabians, Libyans and Iranians. Clement organised an escape in which one of these slaves managed to evade capture and flee from Khartoum.

Clement was suspected and three days later, five masked members of the *Popular Defence Force* (**PDF**) came to his church, assaulted and abducted him.

Clement was taken to one of Khartoum's *"ghost houses"* where he was beaten and tortured daily with electric rods. They repeatedly told him to stop teaching at the church. Clement did not expect to survive the *"ghost house"*. His friends - Emmanual Henry, Peter Malwal and John Bol - had never been seen alive again after their arrests. Yet after seven days, Clement was dumped semi-conscious in the road outside his church - probably as a warning to the others. After recovering from his injuries,

Clement fled from the North and now serves the Lord at the Marial mission station.

Hisim Musa testified of how his village, Krunga Abdullah, was attacked by the PDF in August 1993. The Muslims killed both his parents, burned down all the crops, the houses and the church. They caught one Christian man, Bolis Alhaj, whom they tortured for 3 days before he died. When the villagers fled to the mountains, 124 died from lack of food.

Marcus Kuku described how the PDF attacked their village and dragged Pastor Matta Noor into his burning house. Another man testified of how the PDF attacked his village, Tabanya, burning all the houses and crops, confiscating all their cattle. All the villagers fled because they said that if they were caught, they would have to choose between becoming a Muslim or being killed.

A fact-finding mission team of *Christian Solidarity International* recently returned from Sudan and reported that: *"Humanitarian Aid is failing to reach hundreds of thousands of victims of war and famine. The Government of Sudan continues to refuse to give access to SPLA-administered areas in the Nuba Mountains and to other areas such as Pariang, Nimule, Chukudum, Ikatos, Mundri, and the Southern Blue Nile Region. Denial of access means that thousands of people are dying from lack of food and medicines.*

"Many people in Sudan still suffer from gross violations of human rights. For example, there are reports of recent destruction of villages and of crops. Together with the perpetration of murder and other atrocities by forces in the Nuba Mountains. Many Black Africans, especially women and children, are still subject to enslavement by Arabs from the North.

"The Government of Sudan continues to try to transform, by force, the ethnically and religiously diverse country into an Arab, Islamic state, against the wishes of the vast majority of its Black African population. The devastating effects of this policy are tantamount to attempted genocide.

"The mass displacement of the population of the South and of the Nuba Mountains, by means of terror, war and the manipulation of aid, is the main outcome of this policy.

Twenty-eight army officers were executed in April 1990 24 hours after they were arrested and accused of mounting a coup. (AI)

Conscripts to the PDF training in Kadugli (Nuba Mountains Solidarity Abroad).

"Civil war has created a catastrophe of enormous proportions in Southern Sudan and the Nuba Mountains; an estimated 1,5 million have now died of starvation and disease and over 5 million have been displaced since the outbreak of the latest phase of the war since 1983.

"The war has devastated the infrastructure of these regions, destroying the economic, health, education and communication systems and seriously affecting food production. Offensives by the Government of Sudan forces during last year's dry season inflicted great suffering on hundreds of thousands of people.

"Unless this conflict is resolved as a matter of great urgency, the cost to both the people of Sudan and to the international community will be incalculable . . . There will be even greater demands on the international aid agencies; growing numbers of refugees will pose even greater problems for neighbouring countries; and disease will spread beyond the borders of Sudan.

"The imbalance of military power in favour of the Government of Sudan perpetuates the war and decreases the prospect of a successful outcome of the peace initiatives. Indiscriminate bombing of civilian targets (for example, the areas of Kapoeta and Nimule, January 1995) continues to increase the number of civilians who are killed, wounded and displaced."

The CSI report recommended that the international community take a strong stand against the genocide being perpetrated in Sudan by imposing an arms and oil embargo upon the Government of Sudan and establishing air exclusion zones for the protection of the civilian population from aerial bombardments. The report warned of the GOS tactic of using peace talks *"as a means of buying time to perpetuate its war of attrition"*. In addition, CSI called for permanent access for all humanitarian aid organisations to assist all areas, including the Nuba Mountains. This would also require teams of human rights monitors.

Medical workers in Sudan have reported tens of thousands of deaths due to preventable or treatable diseases. Because of a complete lack of medicines, a large percentage of the population are suffering from meningitis, malaria, whooping cough, TB, bilharzia, Kala-azar (a highly fatal, infectious disease), worms, Sexually Transmitted Diseases and eye diseases.

Dal Magok Deng is a 50-year old man who fled, walking for 4 days, from the fighting at Warrap. He suffered from the cold and from malnutrition and was too weak to move. He could not return home because the PDF would kill him.

Sagol Wek is a 14-year old girl who suffered for 2 years with TB; subsequent complications resulted in osteoporosis of the knee.

Atong Ma Wein, aged 25, and son Maen, aged 3 years, were dying of malnutrition. Her untreated conjuctivitis had caused her to go complete'y blind. Next to this hut were two graves. Her husband and another family relative had both died of starvation.

There were 414 such displaced people in Marial, who had all come to the village when they heard about a food distribution scheme. Unfortunately, the distribution had stopped in September and the people were too weak to return to their own homes, or unable to do so because of the war.

In the midst of this suffering caused by lack of medicines and food, the mission team saw stacks of boxes of chalk provided by UNICEF. Although educational materials are always needed, it seemed inappropriate for such large quantities of chalk to be transported to a place where more basic essentials, such as food, blankets and medicines were so desperately needed that people were dying from the lack of them.

At Nyarweng the only source of water was a pond of filthy water, used by both the cattle and the people. As the villagers tend not to boil the water, many waterborne diseases were being contracted.

The medical assistant at Pariang listed some examples of the tragedies caused by medical shortages:

- A woman with TB and a massive lipoma on one knee: there was no TB treatment available and the lipoma could not be removed, because there were no surgical instruments, suture equipment or dressings;
- A man aged 48, Garang Nuel, blind with cataracts, which could have been treated successfully, if treatment had been available;
- A boy aged 9, Simon Ngor, with an infected wound, which was festering because no antibiotics were available;

– A young mother, aged 28 with two children, aged 6 and 12, both dying of Kala-azar; like so many other people, she had come to Pariang in the hope of medical treatment, but in vain.

The medical workers pleaded for any donations of medicines, surgical equipment or immunizations which could enable them to treat the epidemic diseases which are devastating the people of Southen Sudan.

In the face of such overwhelming needs, our missionaries feel completely inadequate. We cannot meet all the needs - but we can meet some of the needs. And that which we can do - we must do by the Grace of God.

"The Sudanese will raise their hands in prayer to God."
Psalm 68:31 (TEV)

One of many Sudanese who have lost a limb due to a lack of medical facilities.

58

As a bold challenge in the face of the Islamic Jihad, Christians place the cross of Christ on all their dwellings.

Lotuka people gather to receive relief aid.

9

IN THE SUDD

In 1995 a Frontline Mission team conducted a 5 month mission trip to war-torn Sudan. On two occasions they had to be evacuated due to military offensives and once they were evacuated by an emergency medical aircraft after George had a reoccurrence of malaria and Maretha came down with acute pneumonia and dehydration. After recovering they returned to minister in Sudan:

As we walked for hour after hour across the harsh barren plains and severe heat of the Nile Sudd in Southern Sudan, the cross of Jesus was to be seen on the rooftops of all the Christian homes, as we passed through the Nuer villages.

Wherever we stopped, we were welcomed by youth choirs marching toward us with tall, thin wooden crosses before them. The more time we spent with these tall, thin people, the more we were reminded of the words of Jesus Christ: *"If anyone desires to come after Me, let him deny himself, and take up his cross daily, and follow Me." Luke 9:23*

Northern Sudan is predominantly Muslim, while in the South Christianity and traditional African beliefs are in the majority. In the North, Christians face severe repression under the present government policy of Islamic *"Shari'a"* law. While the cross of Jesus is seen as a curse by their Muslim oppressors, it is a symbol of hope and salvation to the Christians of South Sudan and they cling to it wholeheartedly. Although it may mean repression and persecution to them if the Muslims take over control of their village, they are literally taking up their cross and following Jesus for the world to see. As a pastor said: *"Although we are persecuted, we shall carry our cross to show the world that we are Christians."*

Another marsh marathon through the swamps of the Sudd.

A Nuer family in Upper Nile, displaced by the war prominently display their faith with a cross on their dwelling.

"Take up your Cross . . ."

To be a Christian in Sudan often means that you lose your status as a Sudanese citizen, your job, your opportunities to be educated, and even your life. It often means that if you are dying of hunger or disease, you can only receive aid if you deny your Faith and profess that *"Allah is the only true God and Mohammed is his prophet"*.

If you are in a rebel-controlled area, where you are free to worship, being a Christian means that you must choose to no longer take your child to the traditional healers or witchdoctors, although there are almost no medical facilities. Being a Christian means that although you and your family are struggling to survive, you will also share what you have with those who have less. If you are an evangelist or pastor, it means travelling for days on foot, through harsh plains and marshes and across mountains to visit and encourage the believers. It requires something extra, something more, to be a Christian in Sudan. It requires you to take up your cross, deny yourself . . .

"The Lord Added to the Church . . ."

Although Sudan is officially Muslim, and Animism is still widely practised, the Christian Church in Southern Sudan is strong. Despite the difficult circumstances and the war, the Church in Sudan has grown tremendously in the past 20 years: from 5% to 20% of the population.

In Southern Sudan there are 6 main denominations, each operating in different areas: The Presbyterian Church of Sudan (PCOS) in the Upper Nile amongst the Nuer people, the Episcopal Church (ECS) in Western Equatoria among the Dinka and Moru people, the African Inland Church (AIC) in Eastern Equatoria, the Roman Catholics in Bahr-el-Gazahl, the Sudan Pentecostal Church (SPC) and the Sudan Interior Church (SIC). Basically the Catholics and Episcopal are West of the Nile and the Protestants East of the Nile. The biggest growth has been experienced within the Presbyterian and Episcopal churches, where congregations have mushroomed and multiplied so quickly that the training of leaders could not possibly keep up the pace.

Southern Sudan is mostly controlled by rebel forces and the Church is allowed to operate freely in those areas. However, the Christians in those towns and villages invaded and occupied by the Muslim forces are subjected to vicious repression. For many years access to the South has been restricted and closed. In remote areas like the Upper Nile it was impossible for missionaries to reach or enter, but nevertheless the Church grew tremendously. As fighting broke out in different towns, people fled to the rural areas. Wherever Christians fled they started worship services and the congregations mushroomed. In some areas whole Nuer and Dinka villages forsook their traditional animist beliefs and turned to the Lord. Even without Bibles and leaders the Spirit of God has taught His people in Sudan, and we were amazed at the depth of understanding and insight of basic truths of the Gospel. Christians testified of a steadfast trust in the providence of God. According to them, God used the war to spread His Word, and whether they suffer, live or die, they are in the hands of the Sovereign God who is in control of the universe.

Along with this rapid church growth however, the Church has had to deal with tremendous problems and challenges.

There are no training facilities for church leaders in the South, due to the unstable war situation. Most congregations are without trained pastors and are being led by evangelists who often struggle to read and write. Huge numbers of people are turning to the Lord, but they are not being discipled. In some congregations nominalism is a problem. Many of them are pleading for training and teaching. Two men walked for ten days in order to attend the two week seminar which we conducted for church leaders. It took them 4 days just to cross the Nile and surrounding swamps by dug-out canoe! Their desire to know more and be taught in the Scriptures was overwhelming.

Some pastors have been sent out to neighbouring countries to receive training, but most of them have either never returned, or they live in Kenya and just visit their people on occasion. A trained pastor who returns often will have the responsibility of about 80 congregations to care for. One pastor was assigned to an area where there had been no ordained pastor for over 11 years. He disappeared for 14 months, travelling on foot through marshes and rivers, often without food, to visit all the new congregations and baptise believers. He reported baptising more than 9 000 believers!

In "ambush ally" our missionaries passed by a whole column of 12 PDF military vehicles which had been destroyed.

A group of Nuer evangelists praise God for the first shipment of newly translated books of Genesis and Exodus - in their own language!

There is a desperate need for literacy training and Christian literature in Sudan.

"Teach Us to Read"

Another problem is illiteracy. In the war-torn South little education has been available for many years. Christians cry out for literacy training to enable them to read their Bibles. One woman who learned to read testified: *"Now I have found Jesus in the Bible!"* Another asked: *"Now that the Gospel has reached us, how can we teach our children if we cannot read the Bible?"* The translation of the Bible into most Sudanese languages needs urgent attention. Although the New Testament has been translated in a number of Sudanese languages, there is not yet a complete Bible in many of these languages. Old Testament translations into Nuer and Dinka are in the process of being made and we were privileged to witness the first Nuer copies of Genesis and Exodus presented to pastors and evangelists! The Christians celebrated with indescribable joy as they read from Genesis in their own language for the first time!

"I was Hungry . . ."

Of course the desperate physical plight of the people was a constant reality. As we travelled through different areas we saw even worse poverty and misery than what we have seen in Mozambique and Angola. Most of the children were naked and even many adults too.

George ministers to a congregation of Nuer Christians under a shady tree.

*The Presbyterian churches amongst the Nuer in
Upper Nile have experienced phenomenal
growth and revival.*

Hunger is prevalent in most areas, their whole life is a constant struggle for survival. In the far South most people have moved into the mountain slopes in order to escape from the burning down of their villages by either government forces or rebel faction fighting. As a result the women often have to walk up to 4 hours just to collect water from the nearest stream to carry back to their hut.

"Choose You This Day . . ."

In 1964 the Muslim government in Khartoum expelled missionaries from the South. A few managed to remain as relief, development, educational or medical workers, but since the war broke out again with renewed intensification in 1983 most of them withdrew as the rebels took over control of the South. However, a few organisations have returned through Kenya without the consent of the Khartoum government, but with the permission of the rebel authorities.

"No Bibles Allowed"

For the last few years the United Nations have been conducting a major relief programme within South Sudan, although it has been restricted to only those towns permitted aid by the Khartoum government. The United Nations formed *"Operation Lifeline Sudan"* (OLS) as an umbrella under which all relief and humanitarian groups can be co-ordinated. OLS has provided relief and humanitarian aid, and training programmes with regards to education, health and agriculture, as well as basic medical facilities and other development programmes to the Southerners.

However, few of these are Christian-orientated or work alongside the Church. In addition, the UN strictly forbids the transportation of any Bibles, hymn books or any Christian literature at all. The UN have cancelled flights on which they found Bibles and other Christian literature. [*Rather than fly into wherever the UN allows - without Bibles, our mission has chosen not to work under the UN. We prefer to drive or walk into wherever the Lord leads - with Bibles.*]

Different missionary groups are working under the *New Sudan Council of Churches* (NSCC) in close co-operation with local churches of South Sudan. The NSCC broke away from the Sudan Council of Churches in Khartoum as they felt that the interests of the churches in the South were completely neglected. The NSCC is mainly assisting the local churches with relief aid and development programmes, but also co-ordinates missionary efforts, which mainly consist of leadership and theological training. The latter, however, appears to be sadly neglected and inadequate to meet the needs of the churches. We aim to assist these local churches with discipleship and leadership training and with literacy work.

Sudan is a country torn apart by war and it has suffered harsh repression for many years. Yet, little is being done to heed the plight of the Sudanese. Little pressure has been brought to bear on the government of Sudan to change its destructive policies. Peace treaties have been routinely broken as soon as they are signed and yet the world community has remained silent.

A Call to Prayer & Action

Pray for Sudan, make their needs known and work together for the freedom of the Sudanese Christians.

Pray for an end to the devastating war and for the breakdown of spiritual bondage of Islam.

Pray that those who are spiritually blinded, will come to salvation.

Pray for the Church: for an ongoing revival and growth, accompanied by the discipleship of believers and training of church leaders.

Pray for our Christian brothers and sisters to remain steadfast under pressure and repression.

Pray for the church leaders: that they will grow and mature in the Lord, that they will be dedicated shepherds of their flocks despite the difficult circumstances.

Pray for the workers in the field as the fields are white and ready for harvest. You can be involved through your prayers, through your contributions towards the work and through making the situation known.

An Episcopal pastor at a church conference in Moruland.

Part of the crowd celebrating the 5th anniversary of the liberation of Maridi.

10

SLAVERY IN SUDAN

Tens of thousands of Sudanese Christian men, women and children have been kidnapped and sold as slaves by government soldiers and Arab militias. Various research trips by *Christian Solidarity International* to the Nuba Mountains have gathered shocking evidence of the ongoing Islamic slave trade in Sudan:

The thunderous sound of horses made the villagers of Nyamlell drop their hoes and scatter into the bush. Gunfire crackled around the village as 300 men on horseback, camels and on foot crashed through the fields of maize. Clad in turbans and *jalabas* (long white robes) they brandished AK47 and G3 assault rifles, swords and spears. Within minutes the attackers had killed 82 men.

The invaders were Arab slave raiders from the north. Their victims were Dinka Christians. First they siezed the cattle, then they searched from hut to hut gathering food, blankets and slaves. In one hut they grabbed Abuk Marou Keer, a blind Dinka woman. "Now you belong to me" she was told. During this raid the Muslims captured 282 men, women and children from Nyamlell. When 3 men tried to escape from the slave column two were shot and the third had his throat cut. Then several women were selected for gang rape. Even blind Abuk was abused by her captors.

After 2 days forced march Abuk reached a compound which she was told would be her home. Soon she was collecting firewood, carrying water and washing clothes as a slave for her Arab master.

After 2 months of bondage Abuk persuaded her Arab guards to give her a few moments of privacy. She then managed to meet up with her mother and sister who took her by the hand and helped her escape into the darkness! Now they are back in Nyamlell, but Abuk's son and daughter are still enslaved.

Over 5 million people in Southern Sudan have lost their homes and are displaced (internal refugees).

71

One Arab slave trader openly described how marauding gangs of soldiers have regularly swooped down on villages of Christians - killing, looting and capturing as many as possible for slavery. This campaign was part of the Islamic government's campaign to Islamise the South of Sudan. *"The slaves, in most cases children and young women, are taken north where they are forced to provide agricultural labour, domestic work and sexual services against their will"*, reported one CSI team member. *"Slavery is used to debilitate the Christian communities, they are forcibly dispersed and/or imprisoned. They have to surrender and submit to becoming Muslims or they are killed."*

Another Arab slave trader, Ibrahim, described how he has resold 200 African children and young women back to their families. Ibrahim claimed that the raids are organised by the government of Sudan (GOS) which arms the Arab militias and encourages them to attack African villages in the South - keeping the booty and capturing slaves. Some slaves are kept by their captors, most are sold for profit. The train which runs from El Obeid to Wau, arming the GOS garrisons in the South, is used as a slave train on its return journey north transporting those captured by the Arab raiders.

A captured PDF officer, Farjellah Wada Mather from Dufur, testified: *"We were armed by the GOS to fight; we were asked to collect children, sheep, goats and cattle and we used to burn some houses. Whatever was taken belonged to the PDF and was our income."* He said that children who were captured in raids were brought up as slaves by their captors, being used to look after livestock or to do domestic work. He described the significance of the railway from El Obeid to Wau: *"The train comes from the North to the South, taking troops and weapons to the South. When it returns, it returns with people."*

One 27-year-old mother, Ashai Angok Berjok, described how she had been captured with her 2 daughters - 4 year old Ayaar and 9 year old Akec: *"The Arabs came early in the morning. We were captured by Nueri Omer and forced to walk seven days to his home in Dhelem. He raped me along the way. Little Ayaar was tied tightly to the back of his horse. As a result her left leg is now paralysed. At Dhelem we were put inside a big fence without any shelter, with many other slaves. Nueri Omer used me as a concubine. Ayaar and I were saved when my husband came with an Arab dealer. My owner made my husband pay*

72

50 000 LS (Sudanese Pounds) for me and Ayaar. My husband did not have enough money for our 9 year old daughter, Akec, so we had to leave her behind."

Deng Ater Kwany from Path, near Nyamlell recounted: *"My wife and four children were abducted during a raid in March 1994. Three of the children and my wife managed to escape. But my 8 year-old daughter, Abuk, remained behind. She is now kept in Naykata in southern Dafur by a man named Ahmed Ahmed! who bought her from her captor. When I discovered where she was, I went North and tried to get her back by legal means. I opened a case against Ahmed Ahmed at the police station at Dira Dira, and had to pay the police 20 000 LS to do this. A police officer named Abdullah accompanied me to the home of Ahmed. This man demanded 50 000 LS for her release. The policeman said that as he had bought the girl she was his property. I was forced to leave her there where she is badly mistreated by Ahmed's wife who calls her by the Muslim name, Howeh. I also lost the 20 000 LS which the policeman refused to return to me. I had to return home empty handed."*

There is no longer any doubt that slavery is still widespread in Sudan. There are also frequent and consistent reports that slaves are being exported to Muslim countries in the Persian Gulf and to Libya. Many of these captives are beaten, treated brutally and sexually abused. Many are branded like cattle. Slaves who are caught trying to escape are often beaten, mutilated or even murdered.

The research team also documented many other atrocities, acts of torture and instances of aerial bombardment of civilian targets.

They estimate that 1.5 million people have perished and more than 5 million have been displaced and lost their homes out of a population of 8 million (mainly Christian) South Sudanese since 1983. They also noted that the government of Sudan is intimately involved in the Islamicist terrorist network including the Hamas and Hezbollah. Sudan's efforts to subvert the governments of neighbouring Eritrea and Uganda have caused these countries to sever diplomatic ties with Sudan.

Despite official denials that slavery exists, the GOS has armed the nomadic Baggara tribe and encouraged them to raid the Christian South. Slavery acts as both an inducement for PDF militias to attack the South and a weapon of terror to destabilize the South.

73

In an official report (20 February 1996) to the *Commission on Human Rights,* the UN Special Rapporteur on Human Rights in Sudan, Dr Gaspar Biro, presented documentation on the systematic pattern of aerial bombardment of civilian targets, arbitary arrests, detention without due process of law, torture, extrajudicial killings, summary executions, forced removals, forced labour and slavery by the GOS. According to his report the slave trade is most prevalent in Bahr-el-Ghazal and the Nuba Mountains. *"Abduction of southern civilians . . . has become a way of conducting the war."* Dr Biro's report concludes that: *"the abduction of persons, mainly women and children, belonging to racial, ethnic and religious minorities from southern Sudan, the Nuba Mountains and the Ingassema Hills areas, their subjection to the slave trade, including traffic in and sale of children and women, slavery, servitude, forced labour and similar practices are taking place with the knowledge of the Government of Sudan . . . and with the tacit approval of the Government of Sudan."*

The *Middle East Reformed Fellowship* has reported on the abuse of relief aid. Government sponsored relief agencies have used Muslim missionaries from Nigeria, Iran, Pakistan and Saudi Arabia to lure Christians to convert to Islam with promises of regular economic aid only to those who embrace Islam. Those Sudanese who convert are given "conversion certificates" which qualifies them to receive food and medication from Muslim centres. One Protestant evangelist was offered an enormous sum of money and an attractive salary if he converted to Islam. He presented the Gospel as his rejection of the offer.

A prominent Sudanese pastor also expressed his disappointment in *"the growing tendencies of so-called Christian relief agencies to shy away from involvement in evangelism, Bible teaching or Scripture distribution."*

One man expressed what we have heard from many others in similar words: *"We are grateful that you have taken the trouble to come here to see this tragedy and we hope that your words describing our grief will go around the world."*

11

WAR INTENSIFIES IN SOUTHERN SUDAN

During November 1995 I conducted a mission outreach to Sudan and Rwanda. This trip included 11 flights, thousands of kilometres driving (and a fair bit of walking as well), 42 research interviews, visits to 3 orphanages, 4 hospitals, 2 clinics, 2 mission stations and numerous churches.

There were certainly many opportunities for me to examine my motives and question whether God had called me to go to Sudan. Firstly, Nairobi, in neighbouring Kenya, is a tourist trap awash with NGO's (Non-Governmental Organisations) involved with the relief aid industry. Beaurocratic red tape, corruption, wastage and all the other hallmarks of the UN and its ancillaries are enough to make even the most idealistic person somewhat cynical.

Some of the work being done by the NGO's is truly impressive. For example, the World Food Programme has some very skilled ex-Air Force pilots who carry out air drops from the huge C130 air transports. In just 3 runs they can drop 18 tonnes of maize from 300 feet. Triple bagged and secured to wooden pallets, these relief supplies all land within 180 metres of the X marker.

However, such technical precision is seldom accompanied by personal contact or spiritual ministry on the ground. Nor is it any secret as to why the relief aid is done by air and with great haste. When I first made inquiries as to road access to Southern Sudan, there was much surprise. Several relief columns had been ambushed by bandits. It has been a standard tactic of the Government of Sudan (GOS) to arm dissident groups and encourage bandits to destabilise the South. Several Catholic relief workers had recently been killed on the very road we needed to drive in on. As it was it took us 8 hours to drive 120 km over the very bad roads.

SPLA soldiers help a wounded colleague to safety.

Peter with SPLA soldiers in Eastern Equatoria after early morning exercises.

76

One of the towns we visited, Chukadum, had been frequently bombed by GOS aircraft. The charter company that was to fly us out requested an early departure as the GOS were expected to begin bombing after 11 a.m. When I asked how they could be so definite as to the time, the pilot replied that the GOS were very predictable - *"they never bomb before tea time".* Our pilot also mentioned the danger of surface to air missiles and ground fire during flight. *"We've also been shot at by GOS aircraft during unauthorised incursions but ground fire has been more common."* Even the airstrip in northern Kenya, used by relief agencies, had been bombed on occasions by the GOS. In addition, we were warned to beware of the many GOS spies infesting Nairobi and Lokichoggio.

Nor was the Government of Sudan our only obstacle to ministry in Southern Sudan. The United Nations, which co-ordinates Operation Lifeline Sudan under which all NGO's relief agencies and missions need to work, has a serious bias against the Bible. While we were there the UN banned all New Sudan Council of Churches relief flights because one of their ministers attempted to take on board a box of Communion wafers for Eucharist / Lord's Supper celebrations for churches in Sudan! Yet that same flight took in beer and wine for OLS workers! ACROSS (the main Christian relief agency) had also been slapped with a suspension of their flights for attempting to take Bibles into Sudan.

Other missionaries complained of UN interference forbidding them to take in crosses, Sunday School pictures and other religious materials. One missionary couple reported how UN officials had forbidden the showing of the Jesus film in Nuer at Ulang. The SPLA *(Sudanese Peoples Liberation Army)* Commander insisted on the Jesus film being screened to his people - despite the protests of the UN. The same couple remarked at how inconsistent the UN's position on religion was. In Cambodia, where they had previously served, the UN had erected a Buddhist Temple for the refugees (because *"that is their religion").* Yet in Southern Sudan they discriminate against the Christian faith of the population. As one pastor put it: *"It's not that the UN is against religion, they're just against Christianity."*

During one visit to the International Committee of the Red Cross (ICRC) headquarters in Lokichoggio, we found a senior Red Cross official most agitated. The UN had just refused them permission to medevac (medical evacuation by air) 23 war wounded civilians from

77

Church leaders at an Episcopal Church conference in Mundri.

Peter addressing a church conference in the forest.

78

Ganyiel. In blatant disregard for the Geneva Convention, the Government of Sudan (GOS) had refused permission for the flight (without any reason given) and so the UN would not allow the Red Cross to save these casualties. Considering that it was the GOS who had bombed them in the first place, it seemed somewhat ridiculous to ask their permission to treat those casualties which they had failed to kill.

At the ICRC hospital outside of Lokichoggio, I was shocked at the large number of people who had lost limbs. I assumed that these were from landmines but the medical staff informed me that they seldom received any landmine casualties. In fact, all those who had lost limbs in the hospital were gunshot wounds. I was amazed and asked how so many people could have lost legs and arms to gunshot wounds. They then explained that the long distances and the need to first obtain UN / Government of Sudan permission before medevacs meant that by the time the patient arrived for surgery all they could normally do was cut off the infected limb!

On the border of Kenya and Sudan the ICRC hospital at Lokichoggio with 550 beds, is the main hospital for war wounded from Southern Sudan. Patients come from every part of the South and are therefore separated from their families and communities. Although there are a few clinics there is no adequate functioning hospital in the South. The only X-ray facilities for the over 6 million people of Southern Sudan is in that one hospital (which is actually in Kenya). There is a desperate need for medical volunteers to work at the hospital and for a chaplaincy ministry to provide Gospel literature, Christian films, services and counselling to these needy patients.

Our mission trip to Southern Sudan coincided with a major escalation in the 40 year civil war. The Sudanese People's Liberation Army (SPLA) had seized the initiative by launching a series of strategic assaults in Southern Sudan. As a result of these bold new thrusts, serious casualties and defeats had been inflicted upon the Government of Sudan's Islamic forces. Several tanks, artillery pieces and rocket launchers were captured and many villages liberated from the Islamic occupying forces. Most of the Sudanese border with Uganda was seized from the GOS forces. The GOS supported *"Lord's Resistance Army"* in Uganda suffered a crippling blow at the hands of the SPLA with hundreds captured and the rest scattered. The Lord's Resistance Army are a mystical force of

"Christians" who pray five times a day towards Mecca and receive large shipments of weapons from Khartoum. The supply lines to the SPLA from Uganda were thus secured. Then the SPLA renewed their assault on Juba (the Capital of the South) and predicted its fall within the next months. The Muslim government of Sudan was threatening war with Uganda and Eritrea whom they accused of supporting the SPLA. Thousands of GOS troops were being flown into Juba to re-inforce the besieged garrison there. And the bombing of civilian towns in Southern Sudan was intensified.

Good rains throughout the South had resulted in the best harvest in years. Along with renewed relief efforts, this meant that few were starving in Southern Sudan at that time. Accordingly, the SPLA had been able to seize the strategic initiative and regain much of the ground lost to the GOS forces over recent years. Over 90% of South Sudan was now firmly in the hands of the Christian forces. The Government of Sudan's Muslim army was confined to a few besieged garrison towns such as Juba, Kapoeta, Yei and Torit. These were in danger of being overrun by the latest SPLA offensive.

From my contacts with the SPLA it seemed that their morale was extremely high. They could be heard marching or running whilst singing Christian hymns at 5.30 am every morning. Ongoing training was of a fairly high standard. Discipline was evident and their determination to win was exceptional.

The SPLA captured 3 more towns during their latest offensive.

Some were asserting that the tide of war had at last turned in favour of the Christian forces.

That may have been too optimistic. Even if the SPLA retook any of the major towns, could they hold them? Without an air force and without adequate defences against air attacks any town taken would be subjected to severe bombardment. One SPLA Commander apologised to us that they could not guarantee our protection from GOS air attacks. *"We have no more shoulder launched 'Red Eye' missiles. The Arabs know this so their bombers fly high – out of range – when they drop their bombs on us."*

Nevertheless, the GOS forces have failed to achieve much more than a token presence – at great cost – in a few besieged garrison towns. In the opinion of some military attachés with whom I spoke, the war is unwinnable for the GOS forces. The harsh terrain, vast swamps, wide rivers, dense vegetation and rolling hills of the South is ideal terrain for unconventional forces/insurgents. The local population are uncompromisingly opposed to the Arabisation and Islamisation policies of Khartoum. The war is financially crippling the already impoverished, heavily indebted Arab North. The war is unpopular with the GOS forces who seem to lack both the means and the will to win. By way of contrast, the Black Christians of the South are highly motivated and determined to win. It would also seem that the South is beginning to receive some material support from Eritrea and Uganda. There were also speculations that Egypt may be assisting the SPLA forces in some way. The Khartoum regime has certainly made a lot of enemies amongst its neighbours.

Our mission team defied the UN/GOS ban on Bibles and successfully delivered over a thousand Bibles, hymn books, and Gospels to remote congregations and military units in Southern Sudan. The enthusiastic response of the people of Southern Sudan was an eloquent testimony to their love for life and liberty, and a clear rejection of UN / GOS policy.

81

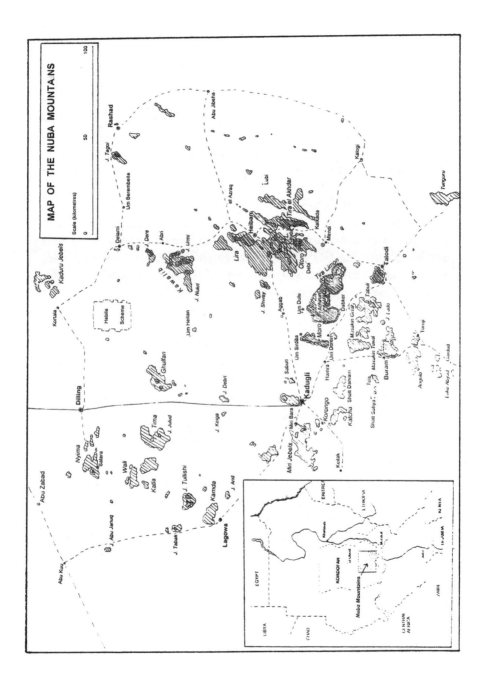

MAP OF THE NUBA MOUNTAINS

12

GENOCIDE IN THE NUBA MOUNTAINS

Since 1985, in the name of Islam, the government of Sudan has maintained a vicious campaign of Jihad against the inhabitants of the Nuba mountains. Some of the very worst atrocities and most intensive battles have occurred in the Nuba.

Geographical Background

The Nuba mountains lie in the centre of Sudan, covering about 30 000 square miles in South Kordofan. The rocky mountains rise sharply 500 to 1 000 metres above the surrounding clay plains. The land - some of it forested and some farmed - is amongst the most fertile land in Sudan. That is both a blessing and a curse to the Nuba.

The Nuba are a cluster of 50 ethnic groups estimated to number 1 200 000 people. There is more linguistic diversity within the Nuba than in the rest of Sudan combined. The Nuba possess a wide cultural diversity - all of which are characterised by a love of music and dancing. Many of the tribes are also known for their body painting, elaborate scarification, wrestling and stick fighting. Most of the Nuba are farmers cultivating the hills in elaborate terraces or the clay plains. Their main crops are sorghum, beans and sesame.

Historical Background

Over the centuries many powerful states have raided the Nuba for slaves. The Nuba retreated to the mountains in order to better resist external invaders. They successfully resisted the Turko-Egyptian armies and the Mahdi's forces. The Nuba also resisted the British vigorously. Between 1900 and 1945 there were over 30 uprisings and rebellions in the Nuba

Burned church in Dabker (Photo: Alex de Waal).

mountains. The first aerial bombardments of the Nuba were carried out on 4 Feb 1926 at Tima and Julud.

Christian missionary activity began in the Nuba in 1874 with some groups such as the Kawalib and Otoro embracing Christianity. While the mystical Sufi sect of Islam has spread widely amongst the Nuba, Christianity has also been on the increase. Christianity has become very attractive to the Nuba youth in particular – precisely because it has been opposed by the government!

Church Burning

The Muslim government began their campaign of church burning in the Nuba in August 1985. The church at Um Derdu was destroyed and 4 Christians killed. The most prominent Christian village, Lubi, was burned down in July 1988. The destruction of churches has become so commonplace that people interviewed by an *African Rights* delegation seldom even mentioned it. When asked if their church was burned during any specific attack the answer always is *"Of course!"*

The leaders of the Episcopal Church in the Nuba Mountains reported to a CSI delegation in April 1996 that the Government of Sudan troops had burned down 26 Episcopal Churches during the past years. At the beginning of 1996 the churches in Toror and Berera were also razed to the ground. Five Episcopal clergymen had been murdered by the GOS forces. Rev Koko from Heiban, Rev Haroun Fadil, Rev John Fadil, Rev Bolis Al Marcus and Rev Anyarko El Haraba from Omdurain. There still remained 7 Episcopalian pastors and 72 churches in the SPLA controlled areas of the Nuba Mountains.

A leader of the Evangelical Church reported that his church, with 2 000 members, has no ordained clergy left in the Nuba Mountains. Two Evangelical catechists, Kamal in Dere and Kabugi in Agar El Ful have been executed by the GOS. The church was also without Bibles.

Gun Control Precedes Genocide

One Christian leader described the process leading up to the wholesale destruction of church buildings and slaughter of Christians:

" In 1985 we were told to register our arms so we could be given ammunition. But it was a trick. All the ammunition was given to the Arabs. And in 1987 the government came and confiscated all the rifles."

From 1985 the military council began to arm the Baggaras (literally "cattle people") - Arab Muslims who live in the Nuba area. This seemed to be a charter for the Arab nomads to become more aggressive and violent towards the Nuba. Sudden attacks, theft of cattle and abductions of the Nuba escalated. A Muslim force called the *Murahaliin* began to forcibly disarm the population, stealing as many cows as possible in the process.

One Christian described the process:

"They had modern guns. We had old guns, marmatons, but we still chased them. The Arabs left and brought the army, and armed themselves more. The government began to attack us and continued attacking us. The problems never stopped."

Resistance

In 1986 a tiny *"Jebels Task Force"* entered the Nuba to recruit for the SPLA. The harsh oppression of the Arabs led many Nuba to join the SPLA. In 1987 the first SPLA fighting force - the *"Volcano Battalion"* entered the Nuba mountains. They won several important battles and secured a substantial area. Nuba youth flocked to join the SPLA and in 1989 the *"New Kush Division"* (six battalions of freshly trained new recruits) entered the Nuba mountains.

The systematic violence of the Muslim government against the Nuba had forced many to turn to the SPLA for protection. The Bashir (NIF) government after the 1989 coup unleashed a ferocious scorched earth campaign. In February 1990 the government called all the chiefs to assemble at Lagowa. All the 14 chiefs who had come, were arrested, bound, and shot by the GOS.

In 1992 the GOS officially declared that *Jihad* (Holy War) existed against the Nuba. Iranian military advisors flew in to assist in the training and deployment of the Mujahidiin. First they instituted a vicious purge within the army, removing all officers who were not considered supportive. Then they unleashed an unprecedentedly large military offensive against the Nuba.

Helicopter gunships, MIG-23 fighter bombers and Antonov aircraft began the aerial bombardment of market places and villages. A massive ground assault on Jebel Tullishi was repeatedly repelled and finally the GOS forces withdrew.

Forced Removals

A massive campaign of forced removals was then launched. Hundreds of thousands of Nuba people were forced at gunpoint to abandon their villages - which were burnt - and they were marched to concentration camps (euphemistically called *"peace camps."*) These unfortunate people suffered appalling hardships without adequate food or medical care over the long forced marches and in the camps where they were finally dumped.

Military Stalemate

By the middle of 1992, the SPLA and the GOS had fought one another to a standstill. The SPLA had repeatedly repulsed the largest series of offensives ever mounted by the GOS. However, the massive deployment of GOS forces had also halted the expansion of the SPLA. The Jihad was not abandoned, however never again did the GOS attempt such massive conventional military assaults. They had lost too many soldiers and such a vast amount of weaponry had fallen into the hands of the SPLA.

For their part the SPLA also had their own problems, mainly due to the August 1991 split in the SPLA where much of the Upper Nile had defected to the Machar/Nasir (SSIM) faction. This cut off the SPLA supply routes to the Nuba. Resupply now had to take the much longer and more hazardous route through Bahr-el-Ghazal. One expedition through this waterless wasteland ended in disaster when half of the 400 men died of thirst. *During the rainy season* another such supply column lost a hundred men drowned in floods.

Kamal Tutu, a Nuba from Al-Atmur al-Negrah was tied up by Muslim government forces and thrown into a burning church. (AI)

"Combing" and Scorched Earth

In February 1993 the worst massacre occurred when the Muslims attacked el Abyad. Over 1 900 civilians were massacred, 12 000 cows stolen and the village and crops burned down.

From late 1993, however, the sheer scale of human suffering had exhausted all concerned. There were no more frontal assaults on SPLA positions and there were fewer large massacres. The vicious *"ethnic cleansing"* of 1992 had been modified to the *"tamshit"* - *"combing"* - strategy of depopulating the rebel controlled areas by scorched earth and forced removals (*"draining the sea to catch the fish"* as one put it). Everything necessary to sustain life was destroyed or removed. *"Pseudo-guerillas"* were also infiltrated for arson, assassination and abduction.

A CSI delegation to the Nuba in April 1996 documented the destruction of three villages: Toror, Teberi and Tendri. The attacks were at midday and were supported by heavy bombardments with artillery and aircraft. As the civilians fled the bombardments, the GOS troops arrived in 8 trucks (3 of them with mounted machine guns) and 1 tank. One eye-witness, Noah, gave this account: *"The enemy first came to Toror, shelling with heavy. artillery and then shelled our village, terrorising the people to flee. When they reached the stream, they opened fire intensively and the grass began to catch fire. Some advanced to the market, others remained stationed behind trees or in the river bed, so they surrounded the whole village. The tank patrolled around. They took our food and burnt what they could not take. They slaughtered the goats, leaving them as carcasses."*

Another victim, Isaac, described what happened:
"When we heard the enemy coming, we scatterd our belongings before escaping. But the enemy collected them and burnt everything: All our 4 granaries, all our 12 sacks of maize . . . the whole village was ablaze. We have no food left. But the neighbouring communities are giving us food. We cannot, we will not move away. This is our village. We are rebuilding before the rainy season starts. We know the intention of the GOS: they want us to go to their Peace Camps. But we will not go. I will stay and rebuild my home and fight if they come again."

The GOS is now pursuing a policy of avoiding military engagements with the SPLA guerrillas. It concentrates all its efforts on attacking defenceless villages and kidnapping, or killing, unarmed civilians. Under the name *"combing"* the GOS army are engaging in the systematic destruction of all villages. Furniture, clothes and household goods are looted. Livestock are stolen. Whatever cannot be carried away is destroyed. Many people have been killed or injured in *"combing"* operations. The GOS forces kill with complete impunity. Old or disabled people who cannot run away are generally shot or burned to death with the village.

"Peace Camps"

Central to the GOS strategy is attracting international assistance to the garrison towns and *"peace camps"*. Since the war began there have been no humanitarian programmes in the SPLA held areas. In contrast, since 1993 some international relief agencies began operating in Kadugli and other government towns, enticing the Nuba people to leave the liberated areas and surrender themselves to be interned in the concentration camps.

In these camps an aggressive Islamisation and Arabisation indoctrination campaign seeks to force inmates to convert to Islam. Children as young as twelve - though most are fifteen or over - are forcibly conscripted into the *Popular Defense Force* (PDF). The *"Peace Camps"* are also used as labour camps - providing a pool of slave labour for the government *"communal"* farms and military projects. Christians have been warned not to gather for prayer or worship. *"If you pray again - you will be killed"* is the common threat. Those who attempt to escape have been subjected to a whole range of penalties from confiscation of all property, including clothes, to torture and summary execution.

The entire *"peace camp"* programme is dominated by the objective of converting the internees to Islam and Arab culture. The only schools allowed are *Khalwas* (Quranic schools).

The GOS strategy is to depopulate the rural areas and provide a captive civilian population in their concentration camps. At present there are an estimated 200 000 Nuba in the SPLA *"liberated areas"* and about

1 million under GOS control in the *"peace camps"*. These *"peace camps"* are concentration camps in the truest sense of the word: the rural population has been forcibly concentrated in these camps to control their movements, to provide a captive population for indoctrination, forced acculturation, forced labour and conscription.

A central component of the genocide is the Sudan government's policy of mass rape. Every Nuba woman who has been in a *"peace camp"* has either been raped or threatened with rape. Girls as young as 9 years old have been raped - with the soldiers justifying this child abuse from the *Hadith* - that Mohammed had married Aisha at 9 years old! Women have been raped as they were abducted, gang raped on arrival at garrisons and repeatedly raped in *"peace camps"* or labour camps, or forcibly *"married"* to Muslim soldiers for the duration of their tours of duty. The aim of this sexual violence and slavery policy has been to destroy the social fabric of Nuba society.

Another component of GOS policy is the strict blockade of SPLA areas. No trade is permitted and no relief agencies have operated there. So far the United Nations and other humanitarian agencies have failed to effectively challenge this exclusion. When cease fires have been called in the South the war has always carried on relentlessly in the Nuba Mountains.

The exceptionally severe human suffering, human rights abuses and persecution of the Christian communities in the Nuba mountains must be the very worst experienced anywhere in the world today. At this critical time the Nuba need the prayers, solidarity and practical support of Christians worldwide.

"Is it nothing to you, all you who pass by?" Lamentations 1:12

A Mosque in Khartoum.

13

THE QURANIC CONNECTION

Only when one studies Islam can one begin to understand the government of Sudan and why the Black Christians in the South are so determined to resist them.

The *Quran* teaches that: men are superior to women (Surah 2:228), a woman is to receive half as much as a man in inheritance (Surah 4:11), a woman's witness in court is only half that of a man (Surah 2:282), women are the possessions of men (Surah 3:14), women are unclean and if a man even touches a woman (even his wife), he is unclean for prayer (Surah 4:43 & 5:6), women should be beaten (Surah 4:34), can be divorced merely by a verbal announcement (but a wife has no such right in the Quran) (Surah 66:5), men may marry up to 4 wives at a time (Surah 4:3), and Allah will forgive a person who forces his slave girls into prostitution (Surah 24:33)!

The Quran teaches that Muslims are superior to others: *"Ye (Muslims) are the best of peoples evolved for mankind. . ."* Surah 3:110

Muslims are forbidden to befriend Jews or Christians: *"O ye who believe! Take not the Jews and the Christians for your friends and protectors. They are but friends and protectors to each other. And he amongst you that turns to them (for friendship) is one of them. . . "*

Surah 5:54

Islam instructs its adherents to fight until all their opponents submit. Christians and Jews may be spared if they pay *"Jizya"* - a penalty tax - with willing submission: *"Fight those who believe not in God nor the last day. . . Nor acknowledge the religion of truth, (even if they are) of the people of the Book, until they pay Jizya (tribute taxes) with willing submission, and feel themselves subdued."* Surah 9:29

"Fight and slay the pagans wherever ye find them and seize them, beleaguer them, and lie in wait (ambush) for them in every strategem (of war); but if they repent and establish regular prayers and practise regular charity, then open the way for them." Surah 9:5 (also 2:193)

For those who resist Islam – execution or mutilation is decreed: *"The punishment of those who wage war against Allah and His apostle, and strive with might and main for mischief through the land is : execution or crucifixion, or the cutting off of the hands and feet from opposite sides or exile from the land. . ."* Surah 5:36

The *Hadith* which is a record of the words and deeds of Mohammed is also viewed by Muslims as inspired. Next to the Quran, it is the most important source of Islamic Law. Its teachings are regarded as binding on all Muslims.

The Hadith teaches that: women are deficient in intelligence and religion (vol 2:541; 3:826), women are an affliction harmful to men (vol. 7:33), women are a bad omen (vol 7:30), and the majority of the damned in Hell are women (vol 1:28, 301; vol 2:161; vol 7:124).

The Hadith also teaches that apostacy is punishable by death: *"Whoever changes his Islamic religion, kill him."* vol 9:57.

A Muslim may not be punished for killing a non-Muslim: *"No Muslim should be killed for killing a kafir (infidel)."* vol 9:50

Those who die in holy war are guaranteed to go to Heaven. *"The person who participates in Jihad (Holy battles) in Allah's cause and nothing compels him to do so except belief in Allah and His apostle, will be recompensed by Allah either with a reward or booty (if he survives) or will be admitted to paradise (if he is killed)."* vol 1:35

In the light of these teachings which are fervently held and propagated by the *National Islamic Front* (NIF) government of Sudan, it becomes clear that the rift between the Muslim Arab North and the Christian Black South in Sudan is too vast. Partition is the only sane answer. The Black South is suffering under the colonial oppression of the Muslim North. Just as Eritrea needed to be set free from Ethiopia; and Latvia, Lithuania and Estonia allowed to secede from the Soviet Union, so too the South should be allowed self determination. De-colonialisation and independence for the South is essential.

Imam Supports Crucifixion

On Thursday, 11 January 1996, an Imam of the *Islamic Propagation Centre International* (IPCI) in South Africa, defended polygamy, jihad and the crucifixion of Muslims who convert to Christianity. This was during a presentation to an international group participating in Frontline Fellowship's *Discipleship Training Course.*

The Director of Frontline Fellowship mentioned that he had recently returned from Sudan where hundreds of Christians in the Nuba Mountains had been crucified by the Islamic government there. The Imam responded that the Quran prescribed the death penalty for apostasy. Therefore, he claimed that any Muslim who left the Islamic religion deserved to be crucified.

At other points in his presentation, the Imam defended polygamy (the practise of having several wives) and Jihad (holy war). The visiting group expressed shock at this blatant disregard for human rights, women's rights and freedom of religion.

In this mosque in Durban, the IPCI Imam declared his support of the death penalty for those who left Islam.

14

CORRUPTION AND DECEPTION – THE UN IN SUDAN

In April 1989 the international community launched Operation Lifeline Sudan (OLS). This initiative was to prevent a recurrence of the 250 000 deaths from war and famine that the country had experienced the previous year.

OLS is an association of the United Nations (UN) and non-governmental organisations (NGO's) pledged to supply emergency assistance to civilians in need, regardless of which conflicting party controlled the area in which they lived. Two of the key founder members of OLS have been the UN Children's Fund (UNICEF) and the UN World Food Programme (WFP). Over 40 NGO's are now linked under OLS which, due to a tripartite agreement between the UN, the Government of Sudan and the SPLA, only serve those areas approved by Khartoum at the time. The Nuba mountains were excluded.

The OLS estimated that 7,5 million people for example were vulnerable to famine, 3,5 million of which lived in the three Southern provinces of Bahr el Ghazal, Equatoria and Upper Nile. Of these 700 000 were considered to be at greatest risk, living on the edge of survival. Another 1,3 million people of the South had fled to the so-called transitional zone, between North and South. An estimated 700 000 displaced Southerners lived in squatter camps outside Khartoum.

Sudan's infant mortality rates were calculated as 102 per 1 000, and for under 5 year olds at 169 per 1 000. Malaria, diarrhoea and acute respiratory infections are common. Malnutrition rates as high as 80% amongst children under five have been reported in some locations.

OLS reported that by 1994 they were moving 140 metric tonnes of food and non-food cargo each day from Lokichoggio into Southern Sudan. More than 10 aircraft were making about 50 take offs and landings each day.

However, despite the impressive statistics, we have repeatedly heard some serious accusations against the UN/OLS from people on the ground in South Sudan. Several NGO's and pilots have said: *"This is a racket. Most of these aid workers don't care about the people in Sudan."* One British NGO claimed: *"Loki is packed full of time-servers getting fat on 5 course meals – with 15 food choices – three times a day."* Several people commented on their shock at the extravagance, gluttony and wastage evidenced at the OLS dining hall in Lokichoggio. As one American relief worker commented: *"This OLS compound in Loki is surreal. There they are within a few miles of serious famine, claiming to be there to feed the starving, while gorging themselves on large quantities of luxury foods and desserts!"*

Other accusations were far more serious: *"OLS is full of blood sucking parasites squandering resources and enriching themselves whilst pretending to aid the starving!"* This English aid worker described the extravagant salaries, excessive living expenses allowances and fabulous fringe benefits as the main reason why most of the relief workers were at Loki. He also gave several shocking examples of wastage and corruption. (Whilst it would be unfair to level these accusations at all aid workers – there must be many sincere and even some sacrificial workers – the incidents of wastage, corruption and callous indifference abound.)

The District Commissioner in Nyamlell complained that for most of the time since the GOS launched an offensive against Nyamlell in March 1995 the area had been designated a *"No-go"* area by the UN. During this attack 82 civilians were murdered and 282 men, women and children captured and enslaved. Yet the wounded survivors were denied any humanitarian aid at the time it most needed such help. When finally, a year later, Nyamlell was removed from the "No go" list hopes were raised that some medicines or food would be supplied at last.

The people were stunned when the UN sent an **empty** Buffalo transport plane (with a 7 ton carrying capacity) in order to take away a pick up truck. Another aircraft came to take away a tractor. Another Buffalo flew in with 7 tons of sand and stone for a water sanitation project. However, in Nyamlell sand and stones were plentiful. The local people were intensely disillusioned with the aid organisations and bitterly disappointed that the re-opening of the airstrip seemed to have resulted in an overall loss of already scarce resources.

Bibles Banned

Many Sudanese Christians complained to us about the UN bias against Christians. The ban on Bibles being transported into Sudan was the most offensive, but they also mentioned many occasions when church related relief flights were cancelled. *"As Christians, we are lower than third class citizens in the eyes of the UN."* Christian organisations such as New Sudan Council of Churches and ACROSS have even been banned by the UN/OLS from having any relief flights for a month - simply for attempting to take Bibles into Sudan!

Partiality Toward GOS Forces

It is also a shocking fact that the Nuba Mountains - which have been the site of the worst atrocities and home to the most desperately needy people in Sudan - have been completely excluded from the OLS relief programme.

Officers in the SPLA also had their own critical observations: *"Under the guise of feeding the starving and suffering Sudanese civilians, the OLS is actually sustaining the Muslim garrison towns."* As another put it: *"There is a great imbalance. Many more OLS planes - and bigger aircraft - fly to the Muslim garrision towns each day than to SPLA held towns. This is how they are maintaining 100 000 Arab troops in the South - the UN is feeding them!"* (He also pointed out that the reported flight schedules were deceptive as flights to Christian towns were routinely cancelled.)

A civilian observer put it even more bluntly: *"The UN is providing the Goverment of Sudan with an efficient air force. The OLS is effectively serving as the logistical support arm of the GOS troops in the South. In this way they are actually prolonging this war."*

Several pastors and NGO's confirmed that the GOS troops in Juba and Wau, for example, had complete control of all relief aid being flown in by the OLS. They maintained that refugees fleeing from these towns report mass starvation while the GOS troops requisition the relief aid. Those civilians who wanted any part of the food aid were forced to convert to Islam. We received multiple testimonies of the abuse of relief aid in Muslim controlled areas. Food aid has routinely been abused as a weapon for enforced Islamisation and Arabisation. Not only are recipients forced to beg for the food *"in the name of Allah"* and recite the Islamic creed, but they are required to change their Christian names to Arabic names!

Those nations and organisations which are funding aspects of Operation Lifeline Sudan should institute a thorough investigation into these accusations of corruption, wastage, anti-Christian bias, mismanagement of resources and the abuse of relief aid by Government of Sudan forces.

> *"The way of peace they do not know, there is no*
> *justice in their paths. They have turned them*
> *into crooked roads; no one who walks*
> *in them will know peace."*
> *Isaiah 59:8*

Hundreds of hands, demanding and desperate, quickly devour the Gospel literature.

15

OVERCOMING OBSTACLES TO SUDAN

Our mission had been invited to present a series of sermons at a Church Conference in Southern Sudan. Thereafter, we were to conduct a Pastor's Training Course and hold various chaplaincy services amongst the armed forces in the area.

As we had a large quantity of desperately needed Bibles and Christian books to deliver to the Churches, we first considered driving overland through Uganda and Zaire. Then word came through of a relief column that had been ambushed on the very road we needed to travel over. This brought to 240 the number of people killed in ambushes on the Northern Ugandan roads in the previous 4 weeks. This was the work of the so-called *"Lord's Resistance Army"* (LRA), which pretends to be Christian but whose members pray five times a day towards Mecca! The LRA has been heavily armed and supported by the Muslim government of Sudan. The LRA's main activities have been attacking the supply lines of the Christians in Southern Sudan. In this, the LRA has been clearly serving the cause of Khartoum. When the Ugandan government closed the Northern roads to Sudan, our only option left was to fly into Western Equatoria.

After a hectic morning in Nairobi, we drove off with flight authorisations for each of our team members to depart at 6am the next morning from Lokichoggio. Estimates of how long the drive would take to Lokichoggio varied considerably - depending on whom one asked - from 6 to 12 hours! As it happened, it took our heavily laden diesel truck 15 hours! The scenic route took us over the Great Rift Valley and through a dozen police checkpoints and army roadblocks. The last 200 km was through bandit territory notorious for violent attacks on cars and hijacking after dark. With our flight leaving the very next morning we had little choice but to press on in faith.

As it happened, all we encountered were stray camels and zebra on the road. When we finally arrived in Lokichoggio at 3 AM, the frustrating task of locating the mission compound from which we were to depart began. When at last we tracked down the compound, we found the people there somewhat edgy. We were informed that their compound had been attacked by armed robbers 6 times in the previous two and a half months, including just two nights before we arrived.

When we finally laid out our sleeping bags it was less than 2 hours to dawn. As it happened, I set my alarm and rose early in vain. The UN had cancelled our flight - without any explanation being given!

The church conference was only 2 days away, so we started driving around visiting various relief organisations, the UN compound and gathering as much research information as possible. By the end of the day, we were seriously praying about chartering a private aircraft to fly our team and Bible shipment in. What made us hesitate was more than just the cost - the UN was warning that the Sudan Air Force had recently stationed 14 helicopter gunships in Juba to shoot down any unauthorised (i.e. non-UN) flights over Southern Sudan.

Breaching the Blockade

As I prayed through the various aspects involved in this dilemma, the Lord's leading became clear. We could not allow our mission to be guided by the UN or the Islamic government of Sudan!

God's people had invited us to this church conference, they desperately needed the Bibles and the Lord had repeatedly confirmed that this mission trip was in His will. No matter what the cost, no matter what the risk, we had to improvise, adapt and overcome all obstacles to fulfill our commitments to the believers in Sudan, breach the UN blockade and deliver the precious cargo of Bibles and Christian books.

We swung into action and by dawn the next morning we were flying into Sudan with the Christian contraband - 1 200 Bibles in 5 languages and several boxes of Christian books and teaching manuals. As we flew over rolling hills, rocky mountains, the wide expanse of the Nile river and adjacent swamps, we were reminded of why aircraft are so important for travel across this vast country.

Christian contraband: 1 200 Bibles in 5 languages were distributed inside Sudan on this one trip.

Soon we were bumping across the bush landing strip. Within ten minutes, the charter aircraft was soaring off again leaving us amidst piles of Bible boxes and our bush kit. We were kindly offered a ride in two trucks to the nearby town, where we were berated by some local official because they had had no prior knowledge of the flight. *"You might have been shot down!"* He was clearly agitated. After calming him down, we were able to begin our journey by road to the site of the church conference.

Camouflaged Church Conference

We were welcomed by an enthusiastic choir of singing and dancing Christians. Speeches were given and a lavish meal prepared. They said that they had scarcely dared to believe that we would be able to make it. It had been many years since they had last had an outside visitor to the churches in their district. We were informed that the battle front – the nearest Muslim garrison – was a mere 15 miles away. Because the last church diocese gathering had been subjected to an aerial bombardment (6 bombs had been strung across the town, one bomb landing in the church compound), they had constructed a special conference venue in the bush outside the town. It was carefully camouflaged under tree cover and would not be visible to Muslim aircraft.

The town was an important centre for spiritual revival and Christian leadership training. The pastors pointed out to us where previous bombs had exploded and the trenches we were to use for cover in the event of an air raid. Every home seemed to have its own trenches for cover.

The next morning an enthusiastic choir and soldiers escorted us through the bush to the conference centre. It was beautifully constructed in a shady clearing covered by tall trees. It was clear that a lot of hard work had gone into this venue. Hundreds of cheerful Christians were converging on the site from all directions. Many were singing, some wore or carried crosses. All looked very happy to see us.

The Commissioner of the district (who is also a church elder) officially welcomed us to the conference. He said that: *"This is a war for religious freedom. The Khartoum government has made it clear that only Islam will be allowed in Sudan."* The SPLA in New Sudan (the South), was fighting for the freedom to hold church conferences like this. He said that they could not guarantee our safety from air attacks but they would do all they could to ensure our safety whilst their guests. Throughout the conference we noticed military patrols circling the area and vigilant soldiers scanning the surrounding jungle.

We learned that all of the people in this town were displaced people. Just a few years ago their town had been overrun by a Muslim offensive. They had then built this temporary town until they could move back to their homes.

We were most impressed with the high standards of civil administration, church structures, community organisation, hygiene and spiritual fervour maintained in the district. The standard of education was high and the incidence of diseases was remarkably low, especially considering the intensity of the war in their district.

The Commissioner explained that the reason for all this was that a Scottish missionary couple – Dr Kenneth Fraser and his wife Eileen – had come and firmly planted the Gospel in Moruland in 1920.

From Scotland To Moruland

Dr. Fraser had run away from home at the age of 14 and had joined the British army. Whilst stationed in South Africa, he was converted to Christ. When his unit was sent to India he met his future wife, Eileen, who was the daughter of an Irish pastor. Eileen had a strong sense of call to pioneer missionary work in Africa and she communicated this vision to Fraser. Soon he returned to Scotland determined to emulate Dr. David Livingstone - so he began to study medicine and theology.

No sooner had Kenneth and Eileen married in 1914, than the First World War broke out. Dr. Fraser returned to the army as a major and was sent to Turkey where he was involved in some of the fiercest battles. By the end of the war he had been promoted to Major General and was much loved and admired by his men. For her part, Mrs Fraser enrolled as a nurse and cared for the war wounded in France.

The Frasers were reunited after the war, completed their training, joined the Church Missionary Society (CMS) and travelled up the Nile to Sudan. They felt led towards Moruland and were welcomed by Chief Yila at Lui on 22 December 1920. The local people, having suffered at the hands of the Turko - Egyptian empire, the Mahdists and Arab slave traders were very suspicious of any foreigners. Within 18 days, Dr. Fraser was presented with a test case - a woman and her child who had been badly mauled by a lion. By God's grace, the patients fully recovered and Dr. Fraser's healing ability was established!

The news spread like wildfire and soon the Frasers had constructed a mud walled hospital to cater for the growing number of patients. By 1926 a new concrete hospital was built. Already in 1921 the Frasers began the first school for boys. These pupils later became the pioneers of education and the church in the country. By 1927, seven of the pupils had qualified to be teachers. They then were sent out to start new schools. Similarly nurses and medical orderlies were trained and sent out.

By the time Dr. Fraser passed away in 1935, he had laid a solid foundation for continual growth and expansion. The Gospels and Acts had been translated into Moru and those he had discipled and trained were vigorously multiplying churches, schools and clinics throughout Moruland.

The Fruit of Faith

The legacy of the sacrificial and far sighted work of the Frasers is still clearly evident today:

More than 80% of the Moru people claim to be Christians.
The largest and most vigorous sections of the Episcopal Church is the Mundri Diocese (Moruland).
* *The highest literacy rate in the country is amongst the Morus.*
The lowest incidence of leprosy and other diseases is in Moruland.
More than half of all the doctors of Sudan are Morus (Most of them are in exile however).
The largest percentage of engineers, artisans, lawyers and politicians in Southern Sudan have come from the Morus.

Pray for these pastors as they each have several congregations to care for.

The Church planted seventy-six years ago by Dr. Fraser has proven to be incredibly resilient - to survive and flourish in spite of severe persecution and debilitating wars.

Today, the Episcopal Church alone in Moruland comprises 24 parishes, 130 preaching centres, 45 pastors, 65 lay preachers and 300 000 church members.

Hunger for the Word

The enthusiastic responses to our presentations from many at the Conference confirmed the vitality of the Episcopal Church in Moruland. And when we brought out a box of Gospel literature to distribute, we were literally mobbed. Hundreds of eager pressing people almost knocked us off our feet as they desperately grabbed some of the precious pamphlets. Seemingly, in no time at all, the large box was emptied and silence descended as the people stood, or sat and carefully read the publications. Some read the messages aloud to eager listeners around them.

Christians converge on the church conference in the forest.

After the Church conference concluded with a joyful celebration of the Lord's Supper, we began to conduct a Pastor's Training Course. Twenty ministerial candidates gathered under the thatch roof of the Church each day from 8am to 3pm to receive instruction in Biblical principles for ministry. They were very grateful for the *Discipleship Training Course* manuals and other resources which we had brought up for them. The question and answer sessions went on for hours - sometimes they invited us to sit around the fire at night and answer their many theological questions.

Each day we distributed Bibles and Gospel booklets to different pastors, teachers and church members in the district. Petrus walked to a remote village of 5 000 people to distribute Bibles and proclaim the Gospel message.

On another day, Rob and Petrus visited the local clinic and ministered to the patients and staff. We also visited a teacher training facility and presented Bibles to each of the trainee teachers. That evening, we presented the Biblical principles for education to the trainees and staff.

On virtually every night of my time in Sudan, I spent the evenings answering questions at fireside discussions. On some occassions, it was with pastors and deacons, on others over a hundred youths crowded around asking many questions ranging from warfare and suffering to sickness and demonic activity. We will never forget the joyful, wholehearted singing around the campfire and the probing questions late into the night. Sometimes only the rain put an end to our discussions. Clearly the people we dealt with in Sudan felt desperately cut off from the rest of the world and were hungry for more knowledge.

The pastors of Sudan desperately need more Bibles and study books.

Some of the youth were despondent about their prospects. They questioned the viability of studying at all when the only education available to them was basic primary school. The devastation and destabilisation caused by the Muslim bombardments and offensives had left only 3 functioning secondary schools in the whole of Western Equatoria (at Yambio, Maridi and Mundri). Most schools had a blackboard but few had much else. Pens, writing paper and textbooks were scarce - many schools having no materials at all. Many of the teachers expressed their frustration that they felt ill-trained and ill-equipped to meet the educational needs of their communities.

The destruction of the economy and infrastructure of the South has drastically reduced the standard of living. Most of the people have only tattered clothes and no shoes. Even the soldiers seldom have uniforms and shoes. We saw many operational soldiers wearing only sandals.

The absence of adequate medical facilities is also keenly felt. Many minor infections and wounds become major problems and even can be fatal because of a desperate lack of medicines and trained medical personnel. Many soldiers have died unnecessarily from wounds because of the great distances which need to be covered before any medical attention at all can be given to them.

The only two hospitals in (SPLA-controlled) Western Equatoria (in Maridi and Yambio) are barely functioning and ill-equipped to cope with surgery. Wounded soldiers and civilians often have to endure a week or more of transportation and waiting before being airlifted to the Red Cross Hospital in Lokichoggio. For this reason, we were requested to bring in medical teams and equipment to assist in surgery and the training of local personnel.

Frontline Fellowship conducts a chaplains period to SPLA troops.

The old military hospital in Miridi had fallen into disrepair and had not been used for many years. As we toured the solidly constructed buildings at the well laid out complex on the hill overlooking Maridi, we could see tremendous potential. It was in quite a state but with gallons of disinfectants and paint and a lot of hard work we could transform it back into an effective medical facility. Then we could invite visiting medical teams to come and assist in training of local staff and care of the war wounded. Many lives could be saved if this hospital is restored.

Celebrating Life and Liberty

On 21 March, we joined thousands of jubilant, dancing and singing citizens of Maridi as they celebrated the 5th Anniversary of the Liberation of Maridi from the Arabs - in 1991. The governor officially thanked those of us who were assisting their suffering people with medical, educational and agricultural projects. We were also told how the Muslim forces had herded civilians at gunpoint and then had them crushed under their tanks as the frustrated GOS forces were fleeing Maridi in 1991.

Soldiers for Christ

The next day, 22 March, we held the first official FF Chaplaincy service amongst the SPLA with a company in Mundri. The captain and his NCO's were immaculately dressed up for this occassion and the clamour for Bibles afterwards was encouraging.

After this we were invited to conduct a Chaplaincy service for the 7th Division at their headquarters in Maridi. We rose before dawn and trekked through the bush and across the town, then up the hill to the barracks. Long before we could see the base we could hear the singing of the soldiers whilst they ran. The barracks were battle scarred with walls pockmarked with bullet holes and torn roofs where mortar shells had exploded.

The unit was in high spirits as they had just heard of the fall of another key town on the Ethiopian border - Pochalla - to the SPLA forces.

Soldiers of the SPLA's 7th Division in Western Equatoria gather to hear Peter at a chaplain's parade.

Approximately 1 500 men of all ranks were gathered on the parade ground singing Christian hymns as the Chaplain - holding high a wooden cross - led them in praise to God for their victory. Many soldiers had crosses pinned to their uniforms. As I presented a Gospel message to the division, they responded enthusiastically. In fact, I had some trouble maintaining the flow of the message as they constantly interrupted with applause and cheers - a very receptive audience indeed.

Afterwards we were mobbed for Bibles and ran out all too quickly. Fortunately we had more boxes back at our camp which we carried over on our next outreaches to the base but even the other 12 boxes of Bibles proved insufficient to satisfy the intense demand for Bibles in their various languages. We need to bring in many more Bibles on our next trips.

"These Bibles that you have brought are a very great achievement" declared the Chaplain. *"We know that it is very difficult to bring them in. The UN and the Arabs do not want us to receive the Word of God because they know that it will be the most powerful weapon for our freedom. This is a great day. These are the first Bibles ever distributed amongst our soldiers. You have been the first foreign visitors to take a Chaplaincy service in the SPLA."*

Medicine for the Soul

I also received permission to distribute Bibles to each of the war wounded patients at the Red Cross Hospital in Lokichoggio. This was an unprecedented and strategic opportunity for ministry. As the ICRC facility is the only hospital for the South Sudanese, patients come from every corner of the war-torn country. After they recover they will be able to return to their areas with their precious Bibles.

I was mobbed by a virtual stampede of patients - many on only one leg or with one arm - desperately pleading for a copy of the Word of God in their own language. Afterwards silence descended upon the hospital tents as the hundreds of patients sat reading their own copy of the Bible - many for the first time.

A Moru Christian rejoices over the Word of God.

16

LOVE IN ACTION AT THE BATTLEFRONT

Increased attacks by the National Islamic Front (NIF) government of Sudan upon the Christians in the liberated zone of Western Equatoria (in Southern Sudan) caused widespread destruction and suffering in 1996. Aerial bombardments forced many inhabitants to flee from the towns. More bridges were blown up, further deteriorating the already dislocated infrastructure and hampering missionary relief efforts. Churches and homes were damaged and destroyed and many Christians killed and wounded in the recent wave of air attacks.

Helicopter gunships attacked and destroyed two churches in Mundri on 23 August 1996. These congregations had been ministered to earlier in the year by Frontline missionaries.

On 17 July, the National Islamic Front government of Sudan forces bombed Mundri – site of the earlier church conference. Six civilians were killed and 28 were wounded. A ground assault on refugee camps in Acholi, Pii and Agago killed 152 people. The Muslim militia and NIF soldiers looted these villages and they raped, tortured and abducted many civilians. The bombings and assaults caused over 60 000 people to flee. For many of the people it was the fourth or fifth time they had lost their homes. Two Episcopal pastors were amongst those abducted by the slave raiders.

A Frontline mission team delivered medicines, Bibles and other relief aid to the area in September. One of the mission team had to be medivaced by air and hospitalised in a neighbouring country.

At the end of 1996, amidst an escalation of the 41 year civil war, with an intensification of bombing raids and a ground offensive by Government of Sudan forces, Frontline Fellowship helped build two field clinics near the battlefront. A shipment of 1 000 kg of medical supplies was delivered, 17 medical orderlies were trained in battlefield first aid

On 23 August 1996, this Episcopal Church in Kotobi was attacked by helicopter gunships and burned to the ground.

and over 8 500 Bibles and Christian books were delivered to the persecuted churches in Equatoria province.

My November 1996 field trip to Southern Sudan had been planned for many months. As I was involved in final preparations an ominous fax came through to our office. Scott had been flown out of Sudan. He was suffering from a severe case of malaria and, according to the doctors, would have died had he not been medivaced and hospitalized.

Diseases and Discouragements

The Frontline team that I had planned to join would therefore not be in the field in November. This posed a logistical problem as the mission's vehicle would also no longer be available. The situation report from the returning field team was also discouraging. They reported that the towns were deserted following aerial bombardments, travel was difficult, a key bridge was down, the roads were bad, there was a lot of military activity and no opportunities for church or chaplaincy services. They had managed to deliver a large shipment of medicines and a fair quantity of Bibles and set up a field clinic for war wounded near the battlefront, but they had not managed to hold any meetings.

The situation was not helped by the fact that our host, Rev. Kenneth Baringwa, was stranded in strife torn Zaire for several weeks (The relief column he was leading lost 5 out of the 12 trucks in the unbelievably bad terrain and took 48 days instead of the expected 2 weeks)! Then our office in Cape Town was broken into and (amongst other things) our fax machine was stolen. This further hampered our communications at this critical stage. Without having received any word from our contacts in Sudan for almost two months, and being unable to communicate with them, several people – recommended that I postpone this field trip.

Complications and Confrontations

The prospects for a productive field outreach in Sudan during November frankly looked bleak. I would be on my own, without a vehicle, in an unstable situation where the previous team had just experienced many frustrations.

The great distances and heavy expenses involved in any trip to Sudan made me seriously question the wisdom of the planned trip. At the same time word came through that two other missionary friends of ours based in Kenya and working into Sudan, had come down with malaria and typhoid.

After earnestly seeking the Lord in prayer, I was convinced that it was the Lord's will that I persevere with the planned mission trip to Sudan. Our Christian friends in Equatoria had been bombed, and some of their churches had been rocketed by helicopter gunships. Some pastors had been abducted and many people had lost their homes and had been forced to flee by the recent offensive. Even if it was not possible to conduct the planned leadership training programmes – I had to go and encourage our friends and deliver as many Bibles as possible.

Few others were convinced that I had made the right choice but I was resolved. The worst situations so often provide the best opportunities for ministry. In fact this proved to be one of our most spiritually successful mission trips ever.

The final days in Cape Town before my departure were predictably hectic. On the eve of the Parliamentary debate on the abortion bill I joined our office staff in a prayer vigil for the right to life of the pre-born outside Parliament. I burnt the midnight oil, completed the latest

Frontline Fellowship News and *UCANEWS* editions, sorted out all the literature, lecture notes and equipment I would need to take and rushed to the airport. It was only 3 weeks before that I had returned from a 7 week speaking tour throughout the USA. I had barely caught up with the backlog of correspondence and the administrative and personnel problems that had accumulated in my absence. I was sad not to be able to spend more time with the family. Our one year old son had just undergone surgery the previous week. As Lenora drove me to the airport she

Bible translators work on the Old Testament in Moru.

informed me that a complication had developed and Christopher would have to go back to the hospital. My mind spun. How could I leave my family at a time like this?

It was with a heavy heart, a racing mind and an exhausted body that I flew out of Cape Town. All I could do was pour out my soul in prayer to the Lord – for His healing hand upon Christopher, His strength for Lenora and for His grace and wisdom to somehow overcome all the obstacles and turn this unpromising trip into one that would glorify God and bless His suffering people in Sudan.

Literature and Logistics

Thanks to friends in America and Germany who had designated a large amount of money for Bibles, Christian books and charter flights into Sudan – I was able to have the long out-of-print *Catechisms* in Moru reprinted and the newly translated *Lay Readers Manual* printed. I was

Some of the pastors and Mothers Union leaders of Maridi Diocese gather for a special combined service at the Maridi Cathedral.

also able to purchase 1 000 copies of the hot-off-the-press new Moru translation of *Genesis* and obtain 1 700 copies of the new Moru book *24 Bible Stories.*

The previous Frontline team had pre-positioned a large consignment of Bibles in Moru, Zande, Bari, Dinka Padang and English near the border of Sudan and to this I now added a further 1 800 Bibles in Madi, Lotuka and Dinka Bor. In addition I purchased hundreds of hymn books and leadership training manuals. But the biggest obstacles lay ahead.

The logistical complications of transporting Bibles into the officially Islamic Sudan is daunting at the best of times. With the war escalating, the infrastructure deteriorating and the hostility of the United Nations to missionary work in general and Bibles in particular – several local missionaries said that it would be impossible at this time.

It was a wonderful opportunity to trust the Lord!

It would take 3 charter planes to fly in all the Christian "contraband". Timing was critical and the co-ordinating of the various people and transports (road and air) needed to obtain the right materials from the different stockpiles of Bibles and books for the successive flights would take more than good planning. There were so many variables and risks involved – it would take several major answers to prayer!

By the grace of God each stage of the operation went ahead successfully. On several occasions I could only praise God for the many faithful and concerned friends whom I knew were praying for this mission. Their prayers were mightily answered.

As William Carey said to his prayer supporters before embarking for India: *"I'm going down into the pit – you hold the ropes."*

Serving the Suffering

The welcome in Maridi was enthusiastic. The Governor of Equatoria expressed his appreciation for the medicines delivered by the previous Frontline team. I was asked to present the sermon at a special joint service in the Cathedral in Maridi. Over 30 pastors and the District Commissioner gathered with the large crowd to pack the Cathedral for this event. The Commissioner also hosted a special public meeting in the Council Chambers where I was invited to address a hundred of the town's elders and intellectuals and to answer their questions. A similar public meeting was arranged in the Kotobi town hall.

Everywhere I received positive feedback on the *Frontline Fellowship News* reports on Sudan and particularly on the **Faith Under Fire in Sudan** book.

Although hundreds had been distributed, it was not enough. Everyone who could read English was most eager to obtain their own copy. They were clearly encouraged that their sufferings and desperate plight were at last being written about and published in the *"outside world."* To see photographs of their own people and situations created quite a sensation.

On several occasions. I was told that they were depending on me to be their ambassador or spokesman to make their persecution known. As the District Commissioner in Maridi put it: *"Peter is an African. His skin may be white, but his heart is black. He is one of us. He speaks for us – as one of us!"*

Soon after arriving in **Moruland** (Mundri Diocese) I was taken on a 20 km hike through the bush to minister to Moru refugees fleeing from the advancing Arabs. The scene at the **Yei** river was heart wrenching. The crowds of malnourished refugees had pitifully few possessions.

117

Destitute Moru families wait for canoes to ferry them across the Yei river to escape the advancing Arab forces.

Many didn't even have clothes left. Across the river I could see large crowds desperately waiting their turn to be transported by dugout canoe. As it was the end of the rainy season the river was full and fast flowing. Only two people could be ferried across at a time in the small hollowed out tree trunks that served as canoes. The fear and desperation was tangible.

For many this was the fourth or fifth time they had lost their homes to a Muslim offensive. Chief Yunamo Iningwa informed me that for 6 consecutive years his people had been unable to harvest the crops they had planted and cultivated. The Muslims chose to attack just before the harvest each year. The people told me of the systematic burning down of villages and the looting of cattle by Government of Sudan (GOS) forces. The administrator of Jambo, Peter Khamis, was publicly tortured by the Arab soldiers. They cut off his ears and broke each finger in both hands. (This happened in September 1996).

Several refugees confirmed that all the Christian civilians – men, women and children – who had been captured by the Muslims in Jambo, Buagui and Lanyi, were made to dig large pits in the ground. They were then forced into these holes which were covered with thorn bushes. The prisoners were then selected at random to be brought out. Those who refused to convert to Islam and/or join the GOS army were tortured by amputations of hands or feet by bayonets.

Some reported that the GOS had used **chemical weapons,** probably gas, to conquer the strategic town of Lui (this was the town where Dr. Kenneth Frazer established the first mission station in Moruland in 1921). At 8:15 am on the 7th July 1996 the GOS dropped 3 bombs on the centre of Lui.

There was an intense fire that burned for 6 days. Several men died, two pregnant women miscarried and all the cattle, chickens and goats in the area died. They reported that the area still looked wet long after the bombing.

On 25 October, GOS troops arrested Pastor Bennet in Yadi. They reportedly tortured him for two days and then took him to Lui. One lady, who was captured at that time and managed to escape, reported that the Arabs announced that they were going to continue targeting pastors because the churches were sending chaplains to the SPLA rebels.

All the churches near Lui had been burnt down and in August helicopter gunships had rocketed two churches in Kotobi.

As one of the pastors commented – it is not true that the ordination of military chaplains had caused the wave of attacks on the churches:

The author with the 17 volunteers who participated in the first Medical Training Workshop, in 1996, outside the first clinic for war wounded established near the battlefront.

119

"The Muslims have been destroying our churches from the very beginning. Anyway the SPLA have never targeted Muslim religious leaders even though they incite the Arab soldiers to attack us."

Kenneth, the Bishop's Commissar for Mundri Diocese and I conducted a church service for the refugees near the river. We distributed New Testaments and Psalms in Moru and the new Moru translation of Genesis and sought to encourage them. Kenneth later returned with two truck loads of food for these destitute people.

Working with War Wounded

The next day I walked to a field clinic that had been set up by Scott. Seventeen military nurses and medics from various units on the battlefront had assembled for a **Medical Training Workshop**. The medics were highly motivated and responded well to my presentations on dealing with the 4 B's: **Breathing, Bleeding, Burns and Breakages.**

Most of the men had previous first aid experience, some had even received medic training in Ethiopia in the 1980's. However they had almost no equipment or medicines. It was a joy to provide the men with some of the medicines, bandages, dressings, drips and equipment that Christian friends had donated in South Africa. The basic training and materials provided would definitely save many lives and limbs. Before I had left they had treated and discharged 20 men with gunshot wounds.

However, there was an overwhelming need for medic bags or backpacks for these field nurses to carry their materials in and more surgical knives, scissors, dressing forceps, dental forceps, iodine, pain killers, local anaesthetics, and antibiotics. They also needed lightweight field stretchers and medical manuals.

The next day I inspected the work in progress at the **Hospital for War Wounded** being restored in Maridi. It was encouraging to see the progress made, much work had been done to clean up the derelict buildings and the operating theatre and pharmacy were already repaired and freshly painted.

On Monday 11th November, we hoisted the Christian flag and held a dedication service for the hospital. All present rejoiced to see the progress and looked forward to the hospital being fully restored and effective in healing the war wounded – body, mind and spirit.

Churches, Colleges and Chaplains

On Sunday 10th November the Episcopal church kept me busy from 8 am to 10 pm. Many pastors had gathered to talk with me before and after the **combined service** in the Cathedral. Then the Youth kept me answering questions till late at night.

The next day I walked up to the military barracks to conduct the **chaplaincy service** for the SPLA's 7th Division. It was encouraging to see the beginnings of a Christian library in the new chaplain's office at the base. Thereafter I conducted a **Pastors' Seminar** for over 70 pastors and theological students. The question and answer session went on till late that night.

The Pastors' Seminar continued the next morning. Then at midday I addressed one hundred of the town's elders and intellectuals in the **Council Chambers**. This was followed by the handing over of compact chaplaincy Bibles to police officers at the Maridi **police station.** We then drove up to **Kotobi.** That evening I led the evening worship with a message from the Bible. Again the question and answer session went on till late. The scene under the stars was spectacular with lightning in the distance silhouetting the trees around us with the brilliant flashes of illumination.

SPLA soldiers patrol near the Yei battlefront.

Bibles and Bombs at the Battlefront

The next day we drove up to **Mundri.** This town has been abandoned because of repeated bombings. (It was bombed again while we were in the area). As it is close to the battlefront only SPLA soldiers inhabited this now otherwise deserted town.

A military escort took us on a guided tour of what once was apparently a beautiful town and a thriving community. The bridge across the *Yei* river had been blown up in several places. The shops and homes were overgrown with vegetation. The Bishop Gwynne College (named after the first Church Missionary Society (CMS) missionary to Sudan) still looked impressive despite having been abandoned long ago. The jungle had taken over the classrooms, chapel and residences – we encountered a green mamba snake in one room – but the structures were solid and could be restored.

I saw lots of shot up and burned out vehicles, shrapnel scarred walls and bomb craters throughout the town. I was also shown some unexploded cluster bomblets.

I was welcomed by two military chaplains and a platoon of joyful Christians singing hymns. The local SPLA commander declared: *"At the beginning of our movement we made a terrible mistake. We forgot something most important. We forgot God. But now we realize that God must be honoured if we are ever to achieve freedom."*

As soldiers gathered for a **chaplaincy service** under the trees, Kenneth expressed his gratitude that the SPLA commander in chief – Dr John Garang – had now ordered that there be prayer parades before any military mobilisation and that every SPLA meeting be opened with Scripture and prayer.

The hymn singing in Moru, Arabic and Dinka reflected the diverse backgrounds of the soldiers. They responded enthusiastically to my message from the Bible and received the Bibles and Christian books with joy and awe.

After completing our ministry amongst the troops in Mundri we set out into the dark, with minimal moonlight, for a rapid 20 km walk (with packs) back to Kotobi. We covered the distance in a brisk 3 hours – with not too much stumbling and falling into potholes!

Tailors at work in the MRDA compound.

Productivity amidst Persecution

The next morning my hosts took me to the burned out Catholic church building. The people there told of how their church had been rocketed and burnt to the ground by a helicopter gunship. Their school which had met in the building was now being held under the trees.

We toured the town and visited the market and some local shops and businesses. Despite the war and extreme poverty of the people the spirit of free enterprise was alive and flourishing. I saw tailors busy sewing shirts and trousers (generally out of used material or sacking materials) and shoe makers crafting sandals out of used car tyres. Farmers were bringing livestock or crops to sell at the market. Builders were constructing huts out of wood, clay and thatch. Teachers were busy instructing their students. Mothers were cooking, washing or cleaning. Some men were digging bomb shelters.

The people I saw there had lost their homes and were displaced, yet there was an infectious joy in this flourishing community and a determination to adapt and improvise. In the afternoon I was invited to address a special meeting with the elders and officials in the town hall. They kept me busy with probing questions for a long time after the message. In the evening I presented a sermon in the Episcopal church

*Pastors all over Moruland rejoice to receive the first of **Genesis** to be translated into Moru.*

compound and answered more ethical, doctrinal, historical and social questions.

Early the next morning 45 pastors and deacons from every part of Moruland assembled for the **Pastors' Seminar.** The District Commissioner of Mundri country officially opened the course in prayer. He also reassured all of us of the steadfast support of his administration for the pastors and of the commitment of his officials to be true to Christian principles.

The pastors were expectant and highly motivated. There was good interaction and they were very responsive to questions. Many won books for accurately reciting key Bible verses by memory. Late that afternoon we officially presented the first copies of **Genesis** translated into Moru. There was much rejoicing. In the evening I was asked many questions – most about Genesis!

Ministering to Muslims

On Saturday I conducted a **Muslim Evangelism Workshop** for the pastors. It was probably the first such course ever run in Western Equatoria.

In the afternoon, shortly after 2 pm, I was busy demonstrating how one could counsel a Muslim to salvation in Christ. Suddenly the sound of bombs exploding in the distance made everyone freeze. Then the distinctive sound of a Soviet Antonov bomber made pastors scramble for cover. The blackboards and bicycles were quickly concealed under trees.

The bomber flew overhead in a wide arc as it circled and flew back in the direction of Juba.

It was a dramatic illustration of how radical Islam evangelises. Their preferred method of reaching out to those who adhere to different religions is through bombings. However, the Bibles we manage to smuggle into Islamic Sudan will prove to be more explosive. Not destroying lives – but rescuing precious people from deception and destruction.

When one compares the Quran and the Bible – it's no contest. The **Bible** is 66 books written by 40 different prophets and apostles, in 3 languages (Hebrew, Aramaic and Greek), on 3 continents (Africa, Asia and Europe), over 1 500 years. The **Quran** is one book, written by one author, in one language, in one geographic area, over 23 years.

Even the Quran acknowledges that **Jesus Christ** was miraculously born of a virgin, was holy and faultless, performed miracles, healed the sick and raised the dead. **Muhammad,** however, was a trader who transported and sold slaves. He was also a slave owner. This we learn from the Muslim's own holy writings – the Hadith. One of Muhammad's

Within minutes of this photo being taken this Muslim Evangelism Worshop was disrupted by the bombing of the nearby town and an Antonov bomber flying overhead.

125

14 wives, Aisha, was only 9 years old when he married her. (According to the laws of most countries in the world that constitutes child abuse.) Muhammad attacked caravans for loot and had over 600 Jewish men in Medina dig their own mass grave before having them all slaughtered. Their wives and children were then sold as slaves. All these facts are recorded in the Hadith.

The authenticity of the Bible as God's revealed Word is attested to by many witnesses, by **miracles** such as the parting of the Red Sea, the fire that came down on Mount Carmel, our Lord   feeding thousands from a handful of food, walking on the water, calming the storm, raising Lazarus from the grave and countless other events.

The Bible contains hundreds of detailed **prophecies.** Our Lord Jesus fulfilled 300 Old Testament prophecies in His life on earth. The Messiah was to be born of a virgin (Isaiah 7:14), in Bethlehem (Micah 5:2), a descendant of David (Isaiah 9:7), 483 years after the decree to rebuild the Temple in Jerusalem (Daniel 9:24-26). He would be betrayed for 30 pieces of silver (Zech. 11:12-13), by a friend (Psalm 41:9), His hands and feet pierced – crucified – (Psalm 22:16), His robe gambled for (Psalm 22:18). He would be buried with the rich (Isaiah 53:9). Yet He would rise from the dead (Psalm 16:10) and ascend to Heaven (Psalm 68:18).

Unlike the Quran, the Bible is convincingly attested to by countless miracles and detailed prophecies.

If you visit Medina you can see the tomb where Muhammad is buried. But if you visit Jerusalem you will find an **empty tomb.** The Lord Jesus Christ has risen! He is the Way, the Truth and the Life. No one comes to the Father except by Him (John 14:6).

The Islam propagated by the GOS is a religion of hatred and slavery based upon a lie. Christianity is a relationship of love with God – based upon the truth.

Article 1 of Sudan's Constitutional Decree (October 16, 1993) states: *"Islam is the guiding religion . . . it is a binding code that directs the laws, regulations and policies of the State..."*

Any Muslim who repudiates his faith in Islam is declared apostate. Under the 1991 Criminal Act, apostasy from Islam is punishable by death.

The preamble to the National Islamic Front (NIF) Constitution declares that its' aim is to group together: *"all the children of Sudan, men and women, regardless of their historical allegiances, their class situation or their regions into one comprehensive organisation working for a Muslim Sudan."*

The government of Sudan provides Islamic religious training to military conscripts and Popular Defence Force (PDF) militia. Near GOS and PDF military bases one can hear the recruits singing of *Jihad,* and the victorious spread of *Shari'a* law.

GOS officials regularly speak in public of the need to transform Sudan into an Islamic state with **one language,** Arabic and **one religion,** Islam. The South needs to be *"brought to the light",* they declare – through conversion, assimilation and abandonment of Southern cultures, their African languages and of their Christian religion.

The war against the Black South is characterized as a Holy War *(Jihad).* The GOS refers to Muslims who die in battle against the South as holy warriors *(Mujahedeen)* and martyrs *(Shu'hada)* and they celebrate their deaths not by funerals but by *"weddings"* as promised in the Quran.

On the 40th anniversary of the independence of Sudan (1 Jan 1996), President Lt. Gen. Al Bashir declared that Sudan was entering a renaissance so that Sudan could perform its Arab, Islamic and

The author presents a Gospel Booklet in Arabic to a Muslim in the Nuba Mountains.

127

Over 8 000 Bibles, Hymn books, prayer books, catechisms and Sunday School books in Moru are divided up between the various pastors for distribution throughout Mundri Diocese.

International roles. He celebrated the spirit of *Jihad* which had engulfed the people of Sudan.

In public speeches, and in his writings, the head of the ruling NIF party, and speaker of the House, Dr al Turabi has often declared his goal of an Islamic empire controlling initially the horn of Africa (Eritrea, Ethiopia, Somalia and Sudan) and later all of East and Central Africa (including Kenya and Uganda). This he refers to as the *Grand Islamic Project*.

That evening the discussion time with the pastors around the camp fire was intense and interesting. They had no illusions that they were involved in a momentous fight for survival. The end of the rainy season always meant a sharp escalation of the fighting. The dry season meant that the Arab armies could move their tanks and trucks. As the water level would drop in the Yei river they were expecting a major offensive from the GOS forces. The bombing was just the beginning.

Christians Celebrate

On Sunday morning people converged for the Episcopal church service. Since their building had been destroyed by the helicopter gunship attack they had been meeting in the forest. It was a bright day bathed in sunshine, hot even in the shade. The colourfully dressed congregation was joined by pastors and guests from all over the district. All the ECS pastors and military chaplains in the district were present for the celebration of the Lord's supper and for worship and the Word.

My heart was deeply touched by the evident love and devotion to Christ evidenced by these faithful brothers and sisters in the Lord. I could only pray that the Lord would mobilise the prayer and support these precious people need in order to achieve peace with justice and freedom to worship Christ.

The afternoon was spent dividing up the thousands of New Testaments and Psalms, books of Genesis, Catechisms and Bible Story books in Moru amongst the various pastors. They rejoiced to receive so much good literature in their own language. The next day they set out on foot to carry their precious loads of Moru Scripture and books to their various congregations.

The evening question and answer session was overwhelmingly concerned with the book of Genesis. When last did you study Genesis? The first time any Moru person could study Genesis in their own language was November 1996.

The aircraft that arrived to fly me out of Sudan also brought in more new Moru books which Frontline Fellowship had sponsored for printing. The Governor and many others came to see me off.

It had been a full and productive field trip: 41 meetings addressed and a total of 3 000 Bibles and 5 500 Christian books in 7 languages had been delivered to over 100 pastors and chaplains in diocese. I had also taken in the 16 mm Jesus film in 3 language: (Dinka, Nuer and Arabic).

"I will lead the blind by ways they have not known, along unfamiliar paths I will guide them; I will turn the darkness into light before them and make the rough places smooth." Isaiah 42:16

17

SERVING THE SUFFERING IN SUDAN

The Frontline Fellowship mission outreaches to Sudan from February to April 1997 were an appropriate way to celebrate the 15th anniversary of our mission.

The logistics were complicated – involving five field workers, a truck, motorbikes, bicycles, several charter aircraft, boats and lots of walking in order to distribute over 18 000 Bibles and other Christian books, in 13 languages, to 6 different regions of Sudan.

The various trips into Sudan were difficult – travelling over some of the harshest terrain imaginable. The heat was stifling – with temperatures of 48°C being recorded in the shade in the Nuba Mountains. The roads were treacherous, we suffered one motorbike accident and one vehicle we were driving needed to be extricated out of a donga. The river crossings were challenging and much of my ministry

United Nations officials enforce the Government of Sudan's ban on Bibles to Southern Sudan.

The logistical challenges of obtaining, stock piling, pre-positioning and transporting sufficient Bibles for these missions to Sudan are considerable.

inside Sudan was accomplished while sick. Scott and Miriam also came down with various illnesses.

The outreaches were dangerous as we had to fly in no-fly zones, in defiance of flight bans, and behind enemy lines. Much of our chaplaincy ministry was completed at the battlefront.

Our team to the Nuba experienced the warm welcome of the government of Sudan and have some of the Muslim tracts (shrapnel from rockets) as souvenirs of this apparently preferred Islamic method of communication!

There were many obstacles which needed to be overcome. After the considerable logistical and mechanical preparations in Cape Town, our team began the 7 000 km drive overland to Sudan. At the first border post, Steve and Scott were harassed and delayed for 23 hours by Zimbabwean customs officials who demanded a 60% duty (tax) on all the (free) relief aid, medicines and Gospel literature being transported to Sudan! By God's Grace our team stood firm and persevered and ultimately bypassed this bureaucratic obstructionism. They travelled over some of the most challenging roads and passed some of the most magnificent scenery.

Medicines and Bibles

Finally, the two Frontline Fellowship field teams to Sudan linked up and distributed over 600 Bibles and New Testaments to the war wounded Sudanese patients in the *International Committee of the Red Cross (ICRC)* Hospital in Lokichoggio. Over a year previously I had received permission from Geneva to distribute Bibles to the Sudanese patients at the ICRC hospital. On that occasion the patients had almost trampled me underfoot as they eagerly and desperately clamoured for their copy of the Word of God in their own language.

Several months later another Frontline Fellowship team had attempted to distribute more Bibles to new patients at the hospital. The ICRC officials explained that the Muslim government of Sudan had complained about the Bible distribution and therefore they could no longer allow it!

As we had some medical equipment to donate to the Red Cross Hospital we were allowed to drive into their compound. While Miriam went off to deliver the medicines, Elton and Scott let some of the Sudanese patients know where they could obtain Bibles. Within minutes Steve and I were besieged by an enthusiastic mass of one legged and one

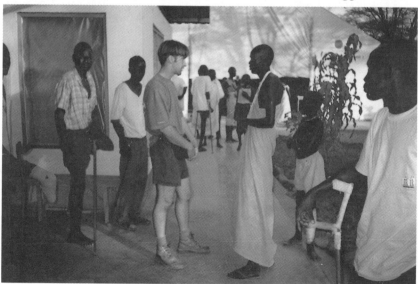

Steve with Sudanese patients at the ICRC hospital in Lokichoggio.

132

armed patients pleading for a Bible in Dinka Bor, Zande, Bari, Nuer, Latuka, Madi or English.

We couldn't distribute the Bibles fast enough. The excitement of the patients was electric. Some of the tall Sudanese men were dancing (on their crutches), raising their newly acquired Bibles high and singing a hymn of praise.

A Dutch ICRC official came to investigate the commotion and was plainly upset. I explained to her that we had come to deliver some medical equipment and when the patients saw that we had Bibles in our truck they had requested their own copies.

"Well, of course they'd want Bibles!" she exploded: *"They're all Christians these Sudanese – all of them!"* This expatriate had a Hindu charm around her neck and was clearly hostile to the chosen faith of the Southern Sudanese. We were requested to leave.

The next day we drove into **Eastern Equatoria** to deliver 500 Bibles to the pastors of Toriet and Bor. At one church we found 12 pastors (representing more than 100 Dinka congregations) providentially gathered together. They warmly welcomed our teams and provided valuable reseach. Each of the pastors looked forward to returning to their congregations with the Scriptures and books we had provided.

Shortly after we returned to Lokichoggio an official from the Red Cross Hospital tracked our team down and urged us to return with more Bibles! Those patients who had not received a Bible were most upset and their discontent had forced the ICRC official to make a list of how many more Bibles were needed in the various languages. Our team promptly returned to the hospital with a futher 136 Bibles – this time by official invitation!

On the night before we flew into Sudan, *Frontline Fellowship* hosted a special supper for the representatives of *Open Doors* and *Voice of the Martyrs*. It was a great time of fellowship and another example of how mission groups need to communicate in order to be more effective.

Throughout the last 17 years Frontline Fellowship has continuously strived to network and co-operate with other ministries. We have recruited and trained many workers for other missions. We have provided vast amounts of photographs and research reports for other missions. We have often taken workers from other organisations into new areas and introduced them to our established contacts. We have organised vast quantities of Bibles and other Gospel literature for other ministries and engaged in many co-operative ventures.

As Steve and Scott prepared for their trip to the Nuba Mountains, Elton, Miriam and I loaded our charter aircraft with over 4 500 Bibles, Hymn and Prayer books and other Christian books. We also took with us an off-road motorbike, two mountain bicycles and equipment, tools and paint for the restoration of a hospital and field clinic. We took off early in the morning while it was still dark. It was an awe inspiring sight to cross the mighty Nile river shortly after sunrise.

There was an enthusiastic crowd to welcome us when we landed in Western Equatoria. There were embraces and lots of handshakes as we exchanged news and sorted out our cargo. The bikes soon came in very useful as we began our varied ministries in the town.

Civil, military and church leaders gathered for the official opening of the *Medical Workshop* where our Registered Nurse, Miriam, was to train 17 medical orderlies and nurses.

Elton organised a team of cleaners, carpenters and painters to repair and restore the **Hospital for War Wounded.** Elton also painted the Chaplains' Office at the military base.

I conducted various chaplaincy services for the local SPLA unit and presented lectures on the Christian Work Ethic and Grace, Faith and

Miriam with some of the medical orderlies and nurses trained at the Medical Workshop in Maridi.

134

As bombing and rocket attacks intensified so bomb shelters became more common.

Works. We also delivered boxes of Bibles and Christian books to local churches, the Bible College, the Chaplains' Office and to the local police and prison.

A Thousand Tongues to Sing

It was a privilege for us to deliver a thousand copies of the new *Zande Hymn Book* to the Maridi Diocese. On a later flight we delivered 2 660 Zande Bibles for the Yambio and Maridi Diocese.

Frontline Fellowship had also sponsored the printing of the new *Moru Hymn Book* and *Moru Prayer Book*. It was a special joy for us to deliver a thousand copies of the Moru Hymn Book and Prayer book to the pastors of Mundri Diocese. There was much rejoicing and many of the pastors publicly expressed their gratitude to those friends of Frontline Fellowship who had literally enabled *"a thousand tongues to sing our great Redeemer's praise"*

We were shown some of the disintegrating remains of the only available previous Hymn and Prayer Books, which had been paperback. They had clearly been well used! The new Hymn and Prayer Books

135

Many of these medics walked for days to participate in Miriam's Medical Training Course.

sponsored by Frontline Fellowship are tough, quality hardcover books – each stitched and bound by hand. These will last for a long time.

On Sunday we conducted 5 services – including a special children's service by the burned out remains of the Episcopal church which had been destroyed by a helicopter gunship attack.

We sorted out the medical supplies and equipment which had been donated by friends of Frontline Fellowship and visited the field clinic which had been established by a previous team.

Twenty-one field medics gathered for the *Medical Training Course.* Many of the medics had walked from the battlefront, several had walked for 3 or more days to participate in the course. Miriam dealt with Vital Signs, Infection Control, First-Aid (Breathing, Bleeding, Breakages and Burns), IV Fluids, Shock, Chest Wounds, Abdominal Wounds, Field Sanitation, Heatstroke, Snake Bites, Injections and Medications.

Elton presented an evangelistic message to the medics and many of them responded by committing their lives to Christ. I contributed some discipleship lectures and Bible studies. On some nights we sat around the camp fire discussing a wide variety of medical and spiritual questions.

Half of the medics had attended the *First Aid Workshop* which I had presented the previous year. Most of them understood English, however the course had to be translated into Arabic for those who struggled.

They related how they have had to stitch up abdominal wounds with ordinary needles and thread – without any anaesthetics, pain killers, antibiotics or anti-inflammatories! It was good to entrust the boxes of medicines and equipment into the hands of these diligent, innovative and battle-proven medics.

At a special service attended by the local civil, church and military leaders, we presented medical textbooks and handbooks to those who had excelled in the course. Badges were awarded to all who passed the written examination.

The commander impressed upon the men that they were the beginning of the new Medical Corps of the SPLA forces. They had a vital responsibility to train others to care for the wounded – whether civilians or soldiers, enemies or friends: *"You must present prompt and efficient medical care even for captured enemy troops. You are to be Christian medics,"* he said.

Straight after the formal conclusion of the course we drove the medics to the new clinic near the battlefront which Frontline Fellowship

The author conducts a chaplaincy service for SPLA soldiers at the battlefront.

137

has helped restore. There we delivered the men with their medicines and held a dedication service for the Field Clinic.

Motorbike Mission

While Miriam was conducting the Field Medic Training Course, Elton and I were travelling each day, often by motorbike, up to the Yei battlefront. There we conducted chaplaincy services and distributed Bibles amongst the SPLA soldiers in the forward trenches.

It was an exhilarating experience to worship the Lord Jesus Christ with hundreds of

An SPLA soldier at the Yei battlefront.

enthusiastic soldiers as they joyfully raised high the newly acquired Bibles and books and cheered. The distinctive Christian flag with the red cross on the blue square on white flapped in the wind as the SPLA soldiers wholeheartedly sang songs of praise.

The commander stepped forward and raised his AK-47 assault rifle. The men chanted some slogan. Then he raised a copy of the Dinka Bor New Testament and the men cheered. As the commander lifted up a copy of *Faith Under Fire in Sudan* the soldiers cheered enthusiastically.

The commander expressed their appreciation for Christian friends who prayed and who spoke up for them in their struggle for survival. *"The Muslim government is trying to destroy the Church,"* he said. *"We are fighting for freedom of religion. We are not only fighting for freedom for Christians but for all people. Not even the Muslims enjoy freedom in Sudan. No Muslim is free to change his religion. We are fighting for freedom for both Muslims and Christians. Freedom to know the Word of God and to obey it!"* It was a special joy to proclaim God's Word to such fighters for freedom.

Unfortunately, I was sick with a fever for the last 2 weeks of this trip, but I could not let that interfere with the wonderful privilege of proclaiming the Word of God to such enthusiastic and receptive people. I just swallowed the medicines and kept pushing myself every day.

Sometimes we could hear the sounds of fighting as the SPLA exchanged gunfire with nearby government forces. On a couple of occasions we heard and saw Antonov bombers flying by. We met with soldiers who had deserted the government forces and come over to fight for the South.

Our ministry in the area coincided with a dramatic new offensive by the SPLA. In a series of bold lightening strikes the SPLA succeeded in capturing the strategic towns of Kaya, Yei, Lainya and Kajo Keji. By the end of March the SPLA had liberated 24 towns and had killed, wounded or captured 16 000 GOS troops. They had also captured a vast quantity of weapons and ammunition, including tanks and anti-aircraft batteries.

The SPLA victories provoked the GOS to place a total flight ban on the area we were ministering in. This presented potential problems for our flights which were bringing in other team members and the next shipments of Bibles.

However, by the grace of God, every one of our varied flights (although all were illegal and risked being intercepted by the GOS airforce) succeeded in breaching the blockade.

A Frontline mission team prepares to cross the Yei river with off-road motorbikes – by boat.

By the end of March we had safely delivered over 11 000 Bibles and other Christian books in 13 languages to 5 regions.

Elton and I, and later Steve and Scott when they had returned from the Nuba Mountains, used the bicycles and motorbikes to good effect. We crossed rivers and fair distances to deliver boxes of Bibles and preach the Word in remote areas.

It was on the return trip from one of these outreaches that Scott and I were injured as our motorbike came crashing down on a treacherous stretch of a rocky road. Scott now had cuts in both of his legs – one from the gunship attack and the other now from the bike spill. I lost a chunk of meat out of my elbow and was bleeding profusely. I most certainly regretted not wearing my customary leather jacket that day! But we still had hours of travelling ahead of us that day, and the sun was going down so we just had to patch up and press on.

Breaching Blockades

Following the completion of our chaplaincy, medical and Bible distribution work in Western Equatoria, Steve, Scott and Elton drove through Uganda to deliver other shipments of Bibles into Sudan. This required travelling with Ugandan military escorts who had to fight their way through various ambushes by the L.R.A. guerillas in northern

The author with SPLA soldiers at the battlefront.

River crossings in Southern Sudan during the rainy season are challenging.

Uganda. They successfully delivered these separate shipments to rejoicing Sudanese Christians in Central Equatoria.

The recent SPLA victories had, at last, opened the road through Uganda for relief supplies and Bibles to be driven into Equatoria. The GOS stranglehold on Western Equatoria had been broken! The ban on Bibles would now be almost impossible for the GOS to enforce.

However, the GOS surrogates in Northern Uganda, *the Lord's Resistance Army* (LRA) still threatened the life-line as they continued their reign of terror and ambushed relief and mission vehicles en-route to Southern Sudan.

Ploughing through the rain in "Ambush Alley" to deliver Bibles to Sudan.

141

18

STRAFED AND BOMBED IN THE NUBA MOUNTAINS

A joint Frontline Fellowship (FF) and Voice of the Martyrs (VOM) mission team to the Nuba Mountains was attacked by Government of Sudan (GOS) helicopter gunships on 4 March 1997.

FF had been invited to join VOM on their first trip to the Nuba Mountains. VOM chartered the DC-3 aircraft and organised the relief packages of medicines, food and agricultural tools. FF supplied 1 500 Arabic Bibles (of which over 800 were delivered on the first flight). Within 45 minutes of the mission team landing behind enemy lines in the war devastated Nuba Mountains, two MI-24 Hind helicopter gunships came roaring over the airstrip.

Over 500 Nuba civilians had come to receive the relief aid and Bibles. There was much rejoicing and excitement. *"You're the first visitors we've ever had in this area. Nobody has ever brought us any aid before,"* they were told.

One of the two Mi-24 Hind helicopter gunships which attacked the missionaries and civilians in the Nuba Mountains. Steve took this picture whilst under fire.

142

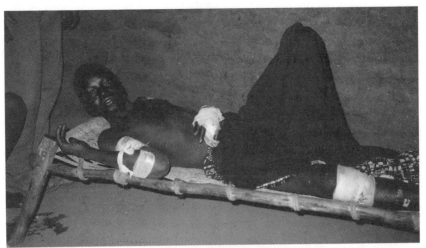

One of the Nuba civilians wounded in the helicopter gunship attack.

They were still organising the aid distribution when the Muslim gunships came in low with twin 30mm machine cannons blazing. As the crowd scattered, one bomb or rocket exploded in the middle of where the crowd had been. The gunships circled and made three strafing runs over the area. They systematically rocketed and shot wherever people were fleeing. Our team saw two Nuba women shredded by machine cannon fire.

More missiles were fired. Huge boulders were blown into pieces. As one MI-24 gunship came roaring across at tree top level with 30mm machine cannons blazing, Scott could actually see the helmeted face of the pilot. The door gunner fired at Steve with a 14.5 mm machine gun. All around Steve the ground was churned up as he sprinted for cover. Bullets cracked and ricocheted alongside as he dived into a dry river bed and took cover.

As Scott ran towards the rocks, something seemed to trip him up and he fell heavily to the ground. Others later said that they clearly saw shrapnel from a missile fly right over him.

One terrified little boy was seen running and screaming as bullets literally churned up the ground all around him. Yet he ran through the gauntlet of flying metal and escaped unharmed. A pastor who witnessed it said that it was clearly a miracle of God's protection.

A Nuba woman who lost her leg in an air attack. The amputation of what remained of her leg had to be done without anaesthetics or pain killers.

Incredibly, only 2 had died in the vicious attack. Considering the vast amount of ordinance expended, it was hard to believe that so few had been hit.

Each helicopter made three or four attacks and left only when it seemed that they had fully expended all their ammunition, bombs and rockets.

Some SPLA soldiers then led the mission team up the mountain to a secure area controlled by the resistance movement. They explained that the Arabs had sent out a mechanised column of ground forces to wipe out our mission team, but the SPLA had ambushed them twice, delaying them effectively.

The local SPLA commander and a pastor welcomed our team warmly. They then organised their people to collect the scattered relief supplies and Arabic Bibles so that the distribution could be effectively carried out.

This was the beginning of an eight day mission to the Nuba. During this time our missionaries saw GOS forces burning dozens of villages and amassed documentation and photographs of the systematic scorched earth *"combing"* policy of the Muslim government of Sudan, their terror bombings, slave raids and concentration camps.

For 3 consecutive days, from 21 to 23 February 1997, GOS Antonov bombers had attacked the villages of Debri, Heiban, Ungurban and Buram counties. From 23 Feb to 2 March, GOS troops (transported by trucks and preceded by T-72 tanks and helicopter gunships) attacked the villages which had been bombed by the Antonovs. All the churches, schools and homes in these villages were set on fire and the livestock either looted or destroyed. On 28 February, nine Nuba women were kidnapped from a watering well at Kawkarya.

Everyday in the Nuba our team heard and saw villages being shelled by GOS artillery and bombed by GOS aircraft. The villages in Heiban country destroyed were: Toda, Elgoz, Nawli, Ere and Andreba (15 000 people displaced). The villages burnt down in Ungurban country included: Tendri, Teberi, Regafi, Kararyia, Garoud El Hemid, Lopa and Lebies (25 000 people lost their homes in this scorched earth campaign). The villages burnt in Buram country were: Tabanya, Lado, Togodo and Romla (12 000 people were displaced from these villages).

When our missionaries asked the Nuba people what their needs were, they listed the following: Education (books and teacher training especially), Bibles and missionaries, clothes, anti-aircraft weapons, bore holes, food and medical supplies.

Our team walked over 120 km, mostly at night, through the mountains and across valleys, between enemy garrisons and past burning villages to reach a secure landing strip in time for an evacuation by air.

Throughout their time in the Nuba mountains, our team was given the most gracious hospitality by the courageous and long suffering Nuba people and the local SPLA unit performed magnificently to protect and aid our missionaries.

Part of the SPLA unit that came to the rescue of the missionaries and escorted them to safety.

19

SPLA OFFENSIVE OVERWHELMS MUSLIM FORCES

A series of co-ordinated military assaults launched by the Sudan Peoples Liberation Army (SPLA) in March 1997 succeeded in capturing 24 garrison towns previously held by the National Islamic Front (NIF) government forces. The spectacularly swift offensive swept all opposition aside and killed, wounded or captured a total of 16 000 enemy soldiers. By the end of March the strategic towns of Kaya, Yei, Lainya and Kajo Keji had been captured by the victorious SPLA forces.

By May 1997, the entire border with Uganda had been secured under SPLA control (as well as the Zaire, Kenyan and Ethiopian borders with

SPLA forces cross the Yei river. The remains of the bridge demolished by the fleeing Arabs is visible in the background.

Sudan). The SPLA's dramatic new offensive broke the stranglehold of the NIF blockade on Western Equatoria and opened the road for relief supplies to be driven through Uganda into Western Equatoria. The SPLA was now also able to link its liberated territories in Eastern Equatoria to Western Equatoria and onto Bahr El Ghazal.

The SPLA offensive began at the end of the dry season, in March, with co-ordinated attacks on Government of Sudan (GOS) garrisions between Kaya (on the Ugandan border) and Yei (the heart of the agricultural belt) in central Equatoria. Just four days later, by 12 March, the SPLA had routed the GOS forces and captured seven GOS garrisons (at Kaya, Bazi, Morobo, Gumini, Limbe, Loka and Yei).

The scale and ferociousness of the SPLA offensive clearly took the NIF regime by surprise. Five days into the offensive and three days after the capture of Yei, the GOS was persisting in promoting the propaganda that they were warding off an invasion by *"Ugandan troops"* at Kaya, but no mention had been made of the SPLA offensive. The GOS vigorously denied that the strategic town of Yei had been captured. The garrison town of Yei was considered so important by the GOS that it was reputed to have had an even larger defensive force than the Southern capital of Juba.

The refusal by the NIF regime to acknowledge that they had lost Yei led to another catastrophic defeat for the GOS. The fleeing GOS garrison from Morobo was informed by radio that Yei was secure and that they needed to break through the SPLA siege of the town. Nearly one thousand GOS troops were killed and a further thousand were taken prisoner by the SPLA in an intensely fierce battle south of Yei as the fleeing GOS force tried desperately to fight their way through to the Yei garrison which no longer existed.

The SPLA captured a vast quantity of equipment from the GOS forces. Seventeen tanks were captured intact at Yei along with an anti-aircraft battery. An Antonov bomber which was sent to bomb Yei was later shot down by this AA battery. The high flying Antonov exploded in mid air.

When finally the GOS admitted that they had *"lost radio contact"* with their garrison in Yei, the NIF leader, Lt. Gen Omar Hassan Ahmad Al Bashir, sought to draw attention away from their humiliating defeat at Yei by claiming that Lainya was his chosen line of defence for Juba.

SPLA soldiers in the forward trenches before the assault on Amadi. The entrenched GOS base at Amadi was overrun after a fierce one hour battle.

Lainya was so heavily fortified that Gen. Al-Bashir even issued a public challenge on TV and radio daring the SPLA to try to take Lainya. However, as he left the TV studios, Al-Bashir was informed that Lainya had already fallen to the SPLA. Lainya had fallen after only a 5 hour battle! The visibly shaken dictator then ordered that all remaining garrisons outside Juba should withdraw into the town itself for the defence of the Southern capital and its air base.

The effect of the news of the unbroken series of SPLA victories was devastating upon the GOS garrisons. As the last remaining garrison town of Kajo Keji was surrounded, GOS troops began to desert in large numbers. When the GOS garrison began its retreat to Juba, it was ambushed and captured along with all their weapons, supplies and equipment. Predictably, the GOS continued to try to cover up yet another catastrophic defeat with another tissue of lies. The official statement from Khartoum claimed that their *"tactical withdrawal"* from Kajo Keji was successful and all had reached Juba safely. The fall of Kajo Keji on 24 March brought to 19 the number of GOS garrisons captured by the SPLA in Central Equatoria since 9 March.

In less than three weeks, the entire military situation had shifted in a dramatic reversal of fortune. Now it was not the SPLA controlled Western Equatoria which was being besieged, but the GOS controlled

Southern capital of Juba! A wave of panic swept through Juba. Morale amongst the GOS troops hit an all time low. Reportedly, many GOS troops simply threw down their weapons and ran or surrendered at the beginning of any firefight.

To compensate for their crushing losses in Equatoria, the GOS mobilised a massive mechanised column in the Upper Nile to capture Maban and Shali on 15 March. To celebrate this victory, the NIF regime announced that a million men would march on the streets of Khartoum to celebrate this great victory. Interestingly, when the SPLA had initially captured Maban two months previously, the GOS radio had informed the public that no such garrison post existed and Maban was merely the name of one of the small tribes living in Upper Nile. By March 15, it had been officially converted into a strategically important town. The mass demonstration in Khartoum, however, failed to materialise.

In fact, the GOS consolation in taking Maban and Shali proved to be rather embarrassingly short lived. On 19 March the SPLA retook both of the towns, captured the garrisons and seized all of the equipment and supplies which had been brought in by the GOS forces. The Commander in Chief of the SPLA, Dr John Garang, reportedly observed that the NIF

SPLA soldiers celebrate the complete destruction of an Arab division at the strategic town of Yei.

"The enemy is my quartermaster!" SPLA soldiers with newly captured weapons prepare to bombard a GOS garrison.

regime had now taken upon itself the task of re-supplying the SPLA. Another leader quipped that Al-Bashir was now acting as quartermaster-general for the SPLA!

Presumably now that the GOS had once again lost Maban, it would be returned to its previous inconsequential status.

By the end of March, over 16 000 GOS soldiers had been either killed, wounded or captured and Amadi, Lui, Lazoti and Jambo had also been captured by the SPLA. The strategic equilibrium in this war between the Muslim Arab North and the mainly Christian Black South had changed with the initiative having been decisively seized by the SPLA.

> *"In that time a present will be brought to the Lord of hosts from a people tall and smooth of skin, and from a people terrible from their beginning onward, a nation powerful and treading down, whose land the rivers divide . . ."*   *Isaiah 18:7*

20

THE VICTORY OF THE CROSS

Amidst a spectacularly successful series of SPLA military offensives in Southern Sudan I delivered a further shipment of Hymn and Prayer books, with medicines, to the persecuted churches. This was the 17th shipment successfully delivered by Frontline Fellowship into war torn Sudan.

Christian Flags Fly Over Newly Liberated Towns

In May 1997, it was my privilege to visit some of the newly liberated areas along the Yei river battlefront. At every town I saw the distinctive (red cross on blue and white) Christian flags flying. There was a joyful atmosphere of thanksgiving to God for the remarkable series of victories the Christian soldiers had so recently experienced. Many soldiers related close calls and answered prayers during the recent battles.

Robert proclaims the Word of God to SPLA soldiers near the battlefront.

151

The graves of the first Christians in Moruland in the foreground and the church in Lui stands as a testimony to the mission work of Dr. Fraser.

Several SPLA officers, including commanders, commented that the turning point in the war was when the SPLA had accepted the appointment of Chaplains and decreed that all parades, and operations were to be started with Bible reading and prayer.

"Our situation seemed hopeless two years ago . . . but as we have turned to God, He has begun to bless us with great victories," declared one officer.

"Each chaplain is worth many brigades of soldiers – they have done a great work in inspiring and strengthening our men," said another.

"These Bibles which you bring," observed one commander *"are very important weapons in our fight for Freedom. **The Christian Bible is more powerful than the bombs of the Muslims!"***

By mid 1997 there were six full time chaplains and 36 chaplains assistants serving in the SPLA. The chaplains reported that hundreds of soldiers had come to faith in Christ in the recent months.

Lui and The Legacy of Dr. Fraser

One of my chaplains services was held in the newly liberated town of Lui. Lui has been a very important and strategic missionary, medical and educational centre in Western Equatoria. It was the birthplace of Christianity in Moruland.

In 1920, Dr Kenneth Fraser, of the Church Missionary Society, travelled up the Nile and felt led to Lui. He was a medical doctor, a teacher, a pastor and also a decorated soldier who had risen to Major General by the end of the First World War.

General Fraser implemented what has proven to be one of the most successful missionary campaigns ever. His strategy was to fulfill the Great Commission by ministering to body, mind and spirit. He started by opening up a hospital, then a school and then a church. Soon he had established nurses training courses, teacher training programmes and pastoral training. He also translated the Gospels and Acts into Moru.

As I stood before the simple white cross which marked the grave of Dr Fraser, I marvelled that what one man started could have accomplished so much. All around me was the evidence: a very large church, large schools, the hospital, the Teacher Training College and the Nurses College.

It was true that the Muslim government bombing and occupation had forced the people to flee and had damaged many of the buildings – but Jesus Christ is the Resurrection and the Life. Christianity is the religion of the empty tomb. Out of death comes life – abundant life.

Laro, the slave traders tree in Lui became the Redemption Tree where the liberating Gospel of Christ was taught.

By 1997 there were over 300 000 Moru Christians who belonged to the Mundri Diocese – for which Kenneth Fraser laid the foundations. Many of the key Christian leaders in Moruland received their education (and often medical treatment too) at Lui.

The signs of the Arab occupation were everywhere – trenches, gun emplacements, pill boxes, mine fields, the debris of war, a newly painted mosque and many vandalised graves. There were a shocking number of broken crosses in the graveyard by the Lui church. (However, I noticed that none of the Arabic signs on the graves of Muslim troops who had been buried in Lui had been disturbed at all.)

Rev. Jeffery pointed out, *Laro,* the huge tree under which Dr Fraser had first begun Bible studies and church services: *"Dr Fraser chose that tree to start the first Moru church because it was the same tree under which the Arab slave traders had bought and sold our people as slaves."*

I looked at the tree with renewed appreciation of God's work of creation which made such a magnificent tree and God's work of redemption (re-creation) which has rescued us from the slavery of sin and death.

We noticed that the memorial plaque which had been set up in front of the Redemption Tree had also been vandalised by the Arab invaders during their occupation.

I preached the Word to the SPLA soldiers at Lui, and prayed with them that the great work begun at that town would continue, that once again the hospital, schools, colleges and church would be fully operating to the Glory of God and for the strengthening of His people in Moruland.

Saving Lives and Limbs

Despite a critical shortage of equipment and medicines, the field medics and nurses who completed the Frontline Fellowship Medical Workshop in March had managed to maintain an operational clinic close to the Yei river. I was most impressed with how much they had accomplished – especially with all the hundreds of patients they had had to care for during the offensives of the previous 3 months.

The clinic was clean, neat and efficiently run. There were over 40 patients in the 4 wards. Most were soldiers with gunshot wounds. A few had been injured by landmines. Some were civilians injured by mines or

Medics at the Mundri Clinic are awarded certificates, armbands and medic packs.

mortars. One man was in a very severe condition. He had multiple fractures and his tongue had almost been severed. The medics had effectively stitched his tongue back together again. (We transported this man back to the hospital at Maridi for further treatment). Some of the patients had various tropical diseases. One 9 year old boy was the only survivor of 3 who had been blown up by a GOS mortar bomb. His mother and brother had already died and he had wounds in each arm and leg and on his body.

The chaplains had organised a special service at the Mundri clinic and well over 200 soldiers and civilians had gathered and were joyfully singing when I arrived from Lui. After some

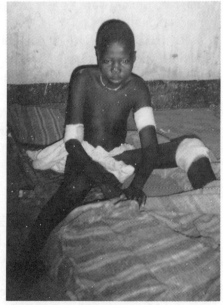

A nine year old boy injured by a mortar bomb that killed his mother and brother.

hymns, prayers and greetings I presented the *Medical Workshop* certificates to those Medics present who had passed the written examination. They also received the first red cross/medical armbands and special medic packs with First Aid materials. In addition we delivered about 700 kg of antibiotics, pain killers, anti-inflammatories, fever reducing agents, bandages, gauze and other vital medical materials which had been donated by Samaritan's Purse.

The Mundri clinic urgently needed sheets (the patients were sleeping on reed mats on concrete floors – there were no beds or sheets and very few blankets available), eating utensils, mosquito netting for the windows, more paint (about half of the clinic has been painted) and of course many more medicines, bandages and gauze. The medics were also looking forward to further training courses and medical teams to come and assist them.

The medical situation in Western Equatoria had become even more critical since the Red Cross had suspended their flights. The Red Cross Hospital in Lokichoggio (Kenya) was at that time, the only fully equipped hospital (with X-ray machines for example) available for war wounded South Sudanese.

The GOS and UN flight ban on most of Western Equatoria also meant that there was no longer any opportunity to fly patients out. This made it even more urgent that we provided the trained and motivated medics in Mundri with all the medicines they needed to alleviate the suffering of the war wounded in Western Equatoria. There were not many places like the Medical Clinic in Mundri where so much could be achieved with so few resources.

Literature Distribution

It was a joy to deliver 1 050 Arabic/English Hymn Books, 240 Avokayo Hymn Books, 2 050 Prayer Books in Moru, 40 Prayer Books in English and two boxes of other Christian books to the pastors of Western Equatoria.

The dramatic advances by the SPLA were also leading to other momentous upheavals as hundreds of thousands of displaced people and refugees started to return to their, now liberated, home areas.

Leadership Training

The Diocese of Mundri was planning to restore the abandoned **Bishop Gwynne College.** This was the largest Bible College and Theological Seminary in Southern Sudan (named after the first CMS missionary to Sudan). As the college had been so close to the battlefront it had been abandoned for the previous decade.

At that time there are only 3 Bible Colleges for all of Western Equatoria – and none of them were in Moruland. The rapid church growth and lack of adequate Bible training had led to a desperate shortage of trained pastors. Frontline Fellowship was officially requested by the pastors of Mundri Diocese to help restore the Bishop Gwynne College. As a most strategically placed leadership training centre – to lay firm foundations for evangelism, discipleship, pastoral ministry and Biblical Reformation.

Defying Flight Bans

On this mission trip, as on many others, the logistics were complicated by a total flight ban by the GOS and UN over most of Equatoria (that part where we are working!) We were told by our hosts that when the

Breaching the blockade: more Bibles are off loaded from a Frontline charter flight.

157

radio message came through that a plane was going to land that day the local officials didn't believe it: *"No planes come here any more. We're under a flight ban."*

Rev. Jeffrey explained: *"No, it's a Frontline Fellowship team coming."* To which they responded: *"Oh! Frontline Fellowship,"* they just nodded. Apparently we have a reputation for routinely breaking UN and GOS rules and flight bans.

The drama that ensued over our return flight was another reminder of just how often we take the Lord's protection for granted on these (illegal) incursions into (the officially Islamic) Sudan. I was walking to the Zande Bible College for the last speaking engagement of my trip when I heard our aircraft – over an hour early. I saw it coming in low and guessed that something was wrong when the pilot landed immediately without first circling the airstrip. I started running and collected my kit on the way.

At the airstrip the pilot was very nervous and impatient to take off. He had been warned by radio that the authorities in Khartoum knew about this flight. The GOS had forwarded official warnings that the aircraft did not have permission to enter Sudan airspace and that it would be intercepted and shot down if it continued. Within seconds we were zooming out at maximum speed at tree top level – straight for the Zaire border. For several tense, prayer – filled minutes we scanned the skies for any sign of enemy aircraft.

By God's grace we reached home safely. It had been another successful trip blessed by God: The Medical Clinic at Mundri was resupplied, the Field Medics had been equipped with First Aid packs, 3 500 more Prayer and Hymn books in 4 languages were delivered, Chaplaincy and Church services had been held, including in newly liberated areas, our friends in Southern Sudan had been further encouraged and important plans and preparations were made concerning future leadership training, educational and medical projects.

21

THE GOSPEL vs JIHAD
IN SUDAN

Sudan is a most strategic country for missions. Sudan is the only country in the Muslim Middle East with millions of evangelical Christians. Muslims have been coming to Christ in Sudan by the thousands. Sudan was the last country to become Islamic. By God's grace it could be the first Islamic country to be won back to Christ!

The Church now faces the final missions frontier of the *10-40 Window* – the block of Muslim, Hindu and Buddhist nations in North Africa and Asia between the tenth and fortieth degrees latitude. Missions to Sudan are on the cutting edge of the great missionary thrust.

During 1997 Frontline Fellowship mission teams made 13 more mission trips into Sudan delivering and distributing over 60 000 Bibles and Christian books in 17 languages inside Sudan.

Steve plunges a Frontline vehicle into another submarine crossing through a flooded river to deliver Bibles to Sudan.

Just during 1997, Frontline missionaries conducted over 550 church and chaplaincy services and leadership training lectures inside Sudan. This included conducting two Medical Training Courses, a Pastors Training Course and a Secondary School Teachers Training Course. Frontline Fellowship teams also delivered tonnes of medical relief aid into Sudan and established a Medical Clinic near the battlefront.

During the last 4 months of 1997, three Frontline Fellowship teams were involved in one of the most logistically complex, challenging and dangerous series of mission trips we had ever undertaken. For one team it involved driving 20 000 km (12,400 miles) overland over some of the most difficult stretches of road, through flooded rivers, through equatorial rain forests in torrential rain, and through the gauntlets of terrorist infested ambush alleys. It also involved flying far behind enemy lines into Central Sudan to deliver a tonne of Bibles to the beleaguered Christians of the Nuba Mountains.

Complicating these outreaches and projects were the political upheavals and civil unrest in countries through which they had to travel in order to reach Sudan. **Zambia** had declared martial law in the aftermath of a failed coup attempt. There were innumerable roadblocks to negotiate. **Kenya** had a state of emergency and regular riots. At one point, riot police had even stormed into churches and beaten up ministers

Off road motorbikes have been invaluable to our work in Sudan.

SPLA soldiers in the forward trenches near Juba prepare for the next offensive.

who had been preaching against corruption. **Uganda** continued to have a serious problem with the LRA terrorist attacks in the North. During one month the LRA murdered 200 travellers on the one road along which our teams have to travel in order to reach the newly liberated areas of Southern Sudan!

And only after overcoming all these obstacles did the real mission begin – of evangelising in the war zones of Sudan!

Mission Impossible?

"Launch out into the deep and let down your nets for a catch."
Luke 5:4

The Lord Jesus ordered Simon Peter to do something he could do – **launch out.** And then He told him to do something he could not do – **fill his nets.** Peter was sceptical – they had worked hard all night and hadn't caught anything. Yet in obedience to the Lord, the big fisherman launched out yet again.

When they had done so they caught such a large number of fish that their nets began to break. So they signalled their partners in the other boat to come and help them, and they came and filled both boats so full that they began to sink (Luke 5:6-7).

This has been our experience in the largest country in Africa, Sudan. When the Lord impressed upon us the necessity of responding to the desperate needs in this officially Islamic country it certainly seemed that we were launching out into **deep waters!**

Since 1955 the Muslim Arab North has been waging a cruel war against the mostly Christian Black South. Since 1964 all missionary work in Southern Sudan has been illegal. The first Frontline mission team I sent up to Sudan came back after 4 months in neighbouring countries and Sudan. They reported that there were no Protestant missionaries in Southern Sudan. No Bibles were available in any of the local languages. The United Nations enforced a ban on Bibles on flights to Sudan. The roads were impossible, especially in the rainy season. The terror bombing of civilian centres was intense. The general consensus of mission groups based in Kenya was that Bible distribution and evangelism in war-torn Southern Sudan was not only illegal, and highly dangerous, but impossible!

I couldn't accept that and so I headed off personally to obey what I was convinced was God's guidance to minister inside Sudan. In neighbouring Kenya I found the big missions who were meant to be inside Sudan had all their people in Nairobi. And the few field staff they had were in Lokichoggio (the UN base in Northern Kenya) which they termed *"the field."*

One mission executive told me that it was *"impossible"* to work inside Sudan. He maintained that the only way to help the Sudanese was by airdrops (rolling pallets of food out the back of C-130 transport aircraft at 300 feet!) *"With a human being you can reason – but not with the Sudanese. They will kill you as soon as look at you. They have no respect for life. It's anarchy in there, a free fire zone."* He was adamant.

It was therefore with great trepidation that I launched out into *"the deep waters"* of war ravaged Sudan. Yet I soon was overwhelmed by the responsiveness of the people to the Bibles we smuggled in and the leadership training courses we presented. The Lord filled our nets to breaking point.

I wrote hundreds of articles and letters on Sudan, spoke hundreds of times on radio and at churches about Sudan and produced videos and the first edition of *"Faith Under Fire in Sudan"*, urging others to join us in ministering to the suffering in Sudan. We praise God that some other missions have responded to the challenge.

Open Doors, Voice of the Martyrs and Samaritan's Purse have also let down their nets and, like us, have found their boats sinking under the incredible, desperate needs. The harvest truly is large and the workers are all too few.

Yes, many bridges are down. The roads are punishing on both vehicles and people. The climate is oppressively hot. The swarms and variety of flying, crawling and biting insects are formidable. There is an ever present threat of malaria, river blindness, guinea worm, typhoid, dysentery and a host of other tropical diseases. High flying bombers and low flying helicopter gunship attacks are very real dangers as are land mines. Bibles are banned. Missionaries are illegal. The country is at war.

Nevertheless, Frontline Fellowship has proven over and over again that it is possible to deliver Bibles, to conduct leadership training courses and minister through church services inside Southern Sudan. As we have launched out in faith, the Lord has blessed our labours with unimaginable success.

Christian "contraband." Tonnes of Bibles had to be loaded and carried across innumerable obstacles and great distances.

We can only praise God for His provision, guidance and protection which have enabled our missionaries to break all records in doing what the experts were all agreed was *"impossible"!*

By ministering to body, mind and spirit, investing in love in action, literature distribution and leadership training, we are strengthening the Christians in Sudan to not only survive the severe persecution, but to win their persecutors to Christ. We are making disciples of the emerging New Sudan.

"Follow Me and I will make you fishes of men."   Luke 4:19

SPLA Advances in the Nuba

After years of desperately fighting for survival in the Nuba Mountains, in 1997 the Sudanese Peoples Liberation Army (SPLA) launched a full-scale military offensive in the Nuba Mountains of South Khordofan. Seven garrisons of the National Islamic Front (NIF) government's occupying force were captured and two concentration camps liberated. With the fall of Bilinia, the provincial capital, Kadugli, came within artillery range of the resistance movement.

In an exclusive interview with the SPLA Commander for the Nuba Mountains, Yosif Kowa Mekki, a Frontline Fellowship mission team was

SPLA soldiers run to confront the NIF invaders.

told that the Nuba people had finally managed to turn their defensive war for survival into an offensive campaign to liberate the long suffering Nuba.

Approximately one million Nubans are incarcerated in the NIF government's *"peace camps"* (concentration camps). About 400 000 Nubans have been holding out in the SPLA controlled liberated areas. The NIF government of Sudan has declared *"holy war" (Jihad)* against the mostly Christian Nubans. Most of the villages in the Nuba Mountains have been destroyed. Most of the churches have been burnt down. Most of the livestock has been looted or destroyed. Even wells have been poisoned. This is all part of the NIF government's scorched earth policy called *"Tamsit"* or *"combing"*.

Commander Yousif Kowa noted that the NIF regime's policy of genocide had only hardened the Nuba people's resistance. In fact the government of Sudan had only succeeded in driving the Nuba people to support the SPLA. If the SPLA succeeds in opening up a land route from Bahr El Ghazal to the Nuba Mountains then the NIF oil fields at Bentiu also will be threatened.

NIF Force Destroyed

An entire mechanised column of NIF government troops was destroyed by the SPLA at the Isoloro Junction in Eastern Equatoria. The military dictator of Sudan, General Al Bashir, ordered the garrison at Torit to recapture the town of Magwe – which the SPLA had overrun in October 1996. General Al Bashir visited Torit on 12 October 1997 to inspect the soldiers before their offensive. This operation was meant to seize the initiative and inflict the first serious defeat on the SPLA in over a year. On 13 October the column left Torit. Twelve km from Torit the NIF force was ambushed by the SPLA and completely destroyed. The SPLA captured two T55 tanks, four 24 tonne Hino trucks and large quantities of weapons, artillery and munitions.

Arabs Bomb their own Prisoners

The high altitude bombing by NIF government Antonovs of civilian centres in the resistance controlled South resulted in 3 Arab prisoners of war being killed and 4 wounded at a POW camp outside Yei on 7 October.

Frontline field workers have been delivering Gospel booklets and Gospel audio tapes in Arabic to the Yei (and other) prison camps.

International Jihad

It has long been known that the NIF government of Sudan receives military support from the Muslim governments of Iran and Iraq. In 1997 it was disclosed that the Muslim states in South East Asia – Malaysia and Indonesia – have also been providing military assistance to the government of Sudan.

A Sudanese diplomat who defected from the Sudan embassy in Kuala Lumpur reported that the NIF has engaged in widespread corruption in order to enlist the support of Malaysia's leaders. Malaysia's national petroleum company, Petronas, now owns a large part of the consortium exploiting Southern Sudan's oil resources. In return Sudan has received a substantial amount of military hardware from the Malaysians. Indonesia recently sent a large military delegation, headed by its Minister of Defence, to Khartoum. This Indonesian delegation actually visited the besieged Southern provincial capital, Juba, to see the desperate plight of their Sudanese allies first hand.

The Indonesians announced that Sudan's Islamic government was *"under threat from the infidels"* and so Indonesia would continue to support Sudan militarily.

During my mission trips throughout Southern and Central Sudan, I have seen the heavy weaponry, including tanks, captured by the SPLA on the road to Juba and have walked over the decomposing corpses, skulls and skeletons of the defeated Arab army. The Christian flags are flying over the newly liberated towns in Equatoria province.

"When you pass through the waters, I will be with you; And through the rivers, they shall not overflow you. When you walk through the fire, you shall not be burned, nor shall the flame scorch you."   Isaiah 43:2

Largest Bible Shipments Distributed in Sudan

From September to November 1997, Frontline Fellowship delivered six shipments of Bibles to seven different regions of Sudan. The number of Bibles and New Testaments, Hymn and Prayer books, Bible study, Sunday School and other Christian books distributed inside Sudan came to 22 086 Bibles and Christian books in ten languages.

The logistics involved in loading and off-loading and carrying over 400 boxes, a total of eight tonnes, across innumerable flooded rivers, over mountains and through swamps in a war zone like Sudan were complex. Often we were caught in torrential rain, slipping and sliding in the mud with boxes of Bibles under tarpaulins. Most of these Bibles were distributed in the newly liberated areas. We reached areas that had never had a visitor before – *"not since the war began"!*

These shipments brought the total number of Bibles delivered to Sudan by Frontline Fellowship in 1997 alone to 36 450. The total number of Hymn and Prayer books delivered comes to 9 765 and other Christian books – 13 790. The overall total of Bibles and Christian books in 17 languages distributed inside Sudan by Frontline Fellowship in 1997 exceeded 60 000!

Three tonnes of Bibles delivered into the newly liberated areas of Western Equatoria – by a World War 2 vintage DC-3.

Return to the Nuba

Over 5 000 of these Bibles, Hymn books and other Christian books were smuggled behind enemy lines to the beleaguered Christians in the Nuba Mountains. In March 1997 a Frontline Mission Team was strafed and bombed by M1-24 Hind helicopter gunships as they delivered Arabic Bibles to this island of Christianity besieged in a sea of Islam.

In September, the same Frontline missionaries, Steve and Scott, returned to the Nuba, walking over 250 km to conduct 30 services and personally deliver 1 200 Arabic Bibles, 1 000 Hymn books and 2 700 other Christian books to 26 different congregations. Often the team was welcomed by singing congregations to escort them to the services.

"How beautiful upon the mountains are the feet of him who brings Good News."   *Isaiah 52:7*

Kotobi Church Restored

In November I conducted the first ever service in the newly restored Episcopal Church in Kotobi. This church building had been destroyed by a helicopter gunship rocket attack in August 1996.

The congregation at Kotobi rejoices over the restoration of their church which had been destroyed by a helicopter gunship attack.

168

Over 500 people packed out the rebuilt church building for a joyous three and a half hour celebration that Jesus Christ is building His Church and the gates of Hell shall not prevail against it (Matthew 16:18)!

Teacher Training Course

An American volunteer, Dr. Monte Wilson, and I also conducted the first training course for secondary school teachers in Western Equatoria since the war began. There are many primary schools in the province, but only three secondary schools. Forty-seven teachers (from each of those three schools) attended this two-week *Biblical Worldview Seminar.*

Frontline Fellowship also provided 1 500 Moru New Testaments and Psalms to 100 primary schools in Mundri County. These Scriptures are now being used as textbooks.

"So shall My Word be that goes forth from My mouth. It shall not return to Me void, but it shall accomplish what I please and it shall prosper in the thing for which I sent it." Isaiah 55:11

Jesus Film in Sudan

Thousands of Sudanese people gathered as Frontline missionaries presented the first screenings of the *JESUS* film in their areas. Evangelists were equipped with Gospel Recordings *"Messengers"* (tough tape recorders with solar panels), Gospel tapes and flip charts. Chaplains were provided with bicycles. Repairs on a Bible College were also begun.

"The Gospel of Christ . . . is the power of God to salvation for everyone who believes." Romans 1:16

Lui Restored

At a special memorial service at Lui, the birthplace of Christianity in Moruland, I had the privilege of presenting the sermon. In it, I paid tribute to pioneer missionary Kenneth Fraser. Dr. Fraser, a CMS missionary from Scotland, brought the Gospel to Moruland in 1920. He established the first hospital, school and church in the area. Twice these buildings at Lui were destroyed by the fundamentalist Muslim government – first in 1965, secondly in the 1990's. Yet on the 15th of November 1997, over 1 500 people packed the Frazer Memorial Church in Lui.

Despite repeated destruction the threefold ministry, to body, mind and spirit, started by Dr. Frazer had once again been restored. The Lui Hospital is fully operational again – over 12 000 patients had been treated and 400 major operations done in the first three months after reopening.

After Lui was liberated from the occupying Arab force, thousands of people came back to Lui and the primary school had hundreds of students enrolled. The resilience of this church has defied all attempts to destroy it.

Jesus is the Resurrection and the Life!

Trench Evangelism

Thousands of Bibles were distributed to SPLA soldiers, including at the battlefront. We travelled by vehicle, motorbikes, boat, bicycle and by foot to deliver Bibles to some of the most inaccessible areas, mostly in the newly liberated territories. On occasion, we literally walked amongst the decomposing corpses, skulls and skeletons of the defeated Arab

Derek shares the Word of God with SPLA soldiers at the battlefront.

170

forces on the battlefield to minister to soldiers in the trenches. Bibles and Gospel booklets were also delivered to hundreds of Muslim prisoners of war.

An SPLA commander remarked how before one battle a traditional blood sacrifice offered by the local witchdoctor was refused by the soldiers who responded: *"We have the Bible, our Christian Flag, our crosses and our chaplains!"* They all knelt down as the Chaplain led the soldiers in prayer. Victory came quicker than thought possible – with few casualties in a battle for a deeply entrenched and heavily mined Muslim government garrison town!

Ministering to Body, Mind and Spirit

At that stage, Frontline missionaries had presented three *Medical Workshops,* the *Teacher Training Course* and four *Pastors Courses.* Through **Love in Action** we minister to the body, **Leadership Training** ministers to the mind and **Literature Distribution** for the spirit.

In so doing we are attempting to follow the example of Dr Kenneth Fraser in ministering to body, mind and spirit.

"Cush will submit herself to God" **Psalm 68:31**

Secondary School teachers in Western Equatoria came together for this Biblical Worldview Course.

171

22

THE LIBERATION OF WESTERN EQUATORIA

By May 1997, the Sudan People's Liberation Army (SPLA) had succeeded in fully liberating the whole of Western Equatoria. The fall of Bo, the last remaining Government of Sudan (GOS) garrison in the province made Western Equatoria the first province of Sudan from which all the National Islamic Front (NIF) Arab forces had been eradicated. The distinctive red cross on blue and white Christian flags were now flying all over Western Equatoria.

The dramatic SPLA offensive, *"Operation Thunderbolt,"* which began on 9 March 1997 defeated several GOS divisions and overran the network of Muslim garrisons, from Amadi and Lui to the important road junction at Jambo to the strategic town of Yei, the key border towns of Kaya and Kajo-Keji, the heavily fortified Lainya and the garrisons at Goja, Boje and Moga.

A Frontline missionary addresses an SPLA chaplaincy service in Western Equatoria.

This successful series of military thrusts was decisive as it firmly placed under SPLA control all the south western approaches to the Southern capital of Juba.

With the beginning of the rainy season the swollen Kit River proved to be a considerable natural obstacle to the further advance of the SPLA forces – especially as the GOS forces had blown up the bridge. During April, however, the SPLA forces, under Commander Mayardit managed to cross the Kit River and launched a series of lightening strikes against four GOS bases. The Arab forces fled in disarray and the SPLA

A joyful SPLA soldier at the Yei river.

advanced to within sight (and shelling range) of Juba.

A bomb crater next to the bomb shelter marks just how close an Antonov bomber came to wiping out the people sheltering there.

The only outposts near Juba still under GOS control were Rejaf and Rokon. Three thousand troops from the defector Rieck Machar's SSIM forces (which had now joined the GOS), which were sent from Upper Nile to help defend Juba, were intercepted and defeated by the SPLA. The SSIM suffered heavy losses and the survivors fled in disarray.

The SPLA offensive had also isolated the besieged GOS garrison towns in Eastern Equatoria, Torit and Kapoeta, which could only be supplied by air drops. These air drops could only be sustained for as long as the Juba air base was able to operate. Juba itself was now cut off, with the SPLA controlling the road routes and threatening the Nile river route from Bor.

Bahr-El-Ghazal and the Red Sea

With the GOS distracted by the threat to their Southern capital of Juba, the SPLA suddenly launched another offensive in May 1997, *(Operation Deng Nhial)* which captured the towns of Tonj, Warrap, Rumbeck and Gogrial in Bahr-El-Ghazal province. Rumbeck fell on 1st May after an intensive one hour battle. Tonj was subdued in just 30 ferocious minutes, a few days later.

At the same time the SPLA, with their new northern allies in the National Democratic Alliance (NDA), also made major advances in Eastern Sudan. The SPLA/NDA Red Sea Offensive overran all the GOS garrisons between Tokar and the Red Sea, including: Algiekh, Atirabi, Migileen, Bitay and Ateek.

Significantly, the tone of the NIF regime's propaganda from Khartoum changed quite dramatically. The NIF spokesmen began saying that their (GOS) forces were *"holding their own"* rather than the earlier *"repelling the invaders"!* The public was being prepared for future defeats and there was a continuous appeal for citizens to enrol in the Popular Defence Force (PDF) militia.

The minister for Information, El Tayeb Mohamed Kheir, was forced to admit that the GOS was facing some serious *"difficulties"* in the East. Kheir stressed that the fall of the threatened Tokar would not mean that (the absolutely vital road, rail and sea lifeline for Sudan) Port Sudan would be on the brink of falling. Because, he noted, Tokar is 200 kilometres from Port Sudan! Observers have concluded that the NIF is apparently depending more upon geographic distances than on any military abilities of its armed forces to protect their dictatorship!

SPLA soldiers at the battlefront study the Word of God.

SPLA forces were also threatening the very strategic railway junction town of Wau in Bahr-El-Ghazal and the hydro-electric power station at the dam near Damazin on the Blue Nile. Reportedly this hydro-electric dam provided more than 80% of the electricity for the national capital, Khartoum.

War Intensifies in the Nuba Mountains

With the liberation of so many key towns in Western Equatoria and Bahr-El-Ghazal, the SPLA will also be able to resupply their beleaguered forces cut off in the Nuba Mountains for over 12 years – once the dry season comes in October/November. Perhaps because of this threat, the NIF forces intensified their efforts to annihilate the Nuba people.

Against all odds, the SPLA in the Nuba succeeded in repulsing six of the eight massive military columns sent into the Nuba Mountains.

However, the two GOS columns which got through devastated many villages, burning crops, vandalising churches, destroying villages, looting livestock and murdering many villagers.

Although the SPLA never discusses its military strategy publicly, one could discern a general strategy of isolating the Southern capital of Juba and preventing any reinforcements or supplies from reaching the beleagured troops of the NIF garrison in Southern Sudan's largest town.

23

WHY DID CHRISTIANITY DIE OUT IN NORTHERN SUDAN?

For one thousand years Christianity predominated in Northern Sudan. From the sixth century to the fifteenth century Christianity was the official religion of the three Sudanese kingdoms of Nubia, Alwa, and Makuria (later Dotawo). For nine hundred years the Christians of Sudan successfully resisted the southward expansion of Islam.

Yet by the late fifteenth century the weakened Christian kingdoms reeled from waves of Arab attacks. Towns were burned and confusion spread. Nubia fell. The fall of the Christian kingdom of Dotawo in 1484 and the fall of the southern most kingdom of Alwa in 1530 heralded the demise of Christian faith in Northern Sudan.

Today Sudan is an officially Islamic state. The National Islamic Front (NIF) regime has declared Jihad (holy war) against the Christian South and against the Arabic speaking Nuba Christians in central Sudan.

Article 1 of Sudan's Constitutional Decree (October 16, 1993) states: *"Islam is the guiding religion . . . it is a binding code that directs the laws, regulations and policies of the State"*. The government of Sudan's leaders regularly proclaim their goal of transforming Sudan into an Islamic state with one language, Arabic, and one religion, Islam.

Nearly two million people, many Christians, have died so far (most from a man-made famine) in the scorched earth and bombing campaign launched by the NIF.

While most of the Black South of Sudan claim to be Christians and steadfastly resist the Islamisation and Arabisation policies of the North, the question still remains:

Why did Christianity die out in the North?

The first Sudanese to be converted to Christ was the treasurer of Queen Candace of the kingdom of Meroe in AD37 (Acts 8:26-40). From this time on Christianity came to be increasingly embraced by the intellectuals and royal households. In Nubia and Alwa the kings seem to have accepted the Gospel first.

The churches in the Nubian kingdom were always closely associated with the king. In fact the king himself was often also a priest and it was a common practice for bishops and priests to hold leadership positions in the government.

There is little historical evidence that the common people were effectively evangelised. As a result, when the kingdoms began to break up politically, the church collapsed at the same time. The church in Northern Sudan was heavily centralised with ecclesiastial heirarchy and a separation between the clergy and the laity.

Even more seriously the churches in Northern Sudan relied heavily upon the services of foreign bishops and priests. Most of the leaders of the church were Egyptian, Greek or Coptic. These languages were understood by the king and the educated people in his court – but not by the common people. Hence, Christianity in Northern Sudan was a religion of the educated elite and not of the common man. The churches were also strong in the towns and cities but had far less of an impact amongst the rural farming communities.

The over-dependence of Northern Sudan on foreign bishops and priests later starved the church of leadership as the Muslim armies cut off all contact between Egypt and Nubia in the thirteenth century. As the Bishops had been appointed by the Greek and Coptic patriarchs in Egypt the Islamic stranglehold made it very difficult for the church in Nubia to continue to grow.

Simultaneously the continuous migration of Arab traders and nomads into Sudan eroded the Christian dominance and spread the influence of Islam. The last years of the Christian kingdoms were years of confusion.

Intermarriage with Muslims brought dissention. The treacherous compromise of the Nubian kings to sell slaves to the Muslims as part of a peace treaty undermined the Christian civilisation which had thrived for nearly a millenium.

There was much quarrelling and conflict within the royal families. The Mamluk rulers in Egypt eagerly interfered and exploited the divisions in Nubia. The churches were so closely connected with the kings and to the patriarchs of Alexandria (in Egypt) that they rose and fell with them.

Another contributing factor to the demise of Christianity in Northern Sudan is that the Christians in Ethiopia refused to send help when asked to. In 1450 six men from Alwa came as Ambassadors to the king of neighbouring Ethiopia. They begged him to send them priests and monks to teach them. Yet this desperate cry for help was ignored.

Christianity did not die out in Northern Sudan because of external persecution by Muslims. The churches were empty and abandoned long before Islam filled the vacuum and became well established. The fact that few Nubians were literate and that services were in Greek and Coptic meant that the Word of God was not well known amongst the common people. The over-dependance upon foreign bishops and priests made the churches vulnerable when communication links to the outside world were cut.

The churches were too closely allied to the political power structures and fell with the kings. By compromising with Islam and allowing a quota of their own people to be enslaved in order to buy assurances of peace the Nubian kingdom condemned itself to be judged by God.

The author with a Coptic congregation in the Nuba Mountains.

Town officials and elders in Kotobi gather to study Biblical principles for government.

The lessons to us today are clear: It is essential that we give priority to literacy training, Bible teaching and leadership training. We need to build healthy self supporting, self governing and self propogating churches. We need to teach and practice decentralisation and the priesthood of all believers.

And we need to be very careful not to be co-opted by secular politicians, only to be used to advance their humanist agendas. Nor may we ever compromise our Faith in order to buy some temporary illusion of peace.

May God be merciful to us and keep us from repeating the errors of the past. Let us be faithful to His Word and to His work. And may we not fail those who are being persecuted for their faith and who are looking to us for help today.

"Cush will submit herself to God."   ***Psalm 68:31***

24

JIHAD – ISLAMIC HOLY WAR

The relentless and often vicious persecution by Muslims against Christians is seldom recognised or understood.

Many assume that the concept of *Jihad,* or holy war, espoused by Muslim leaders like the Aytollah Khomeini was an aberration not truly representative of Islam:

> *"We shall export our revolution, to the whole world. Until the cry* ***'Allah Akbar'*** *resounds over the whole world. There will be struggle. There will be Jihad . . . Islam is the religion of militant individuals . . . Islam will be victorious in all the countries of the world, and Islam and the teachings of the Quran will prevail all over the world . . . This is the duty that all Muslims must fulfill . . ."*
> These were the often repeated public pronouncements of the Ayatollah Khomeini after the revolution in Iran in 1979 (Quoted from *"The Blood of the Moon"* by George Grant).

An Arab trader in the Nuba Mountains.

180

Sharia law being enforced by the Mahdi.

Nor was the Ayatollah alone in such militant threats. Abdul Aziz Ibn Saud declared:

> *"We shall never call for or accept a negotiated peace. We shall only accept war – Jihad – the holy war. We have resolved to drench the lands of Palestine and Arabia with the blood of the infidels or to accept Martyrdom for the glory of Allah."*

The President of Sudan, Lt. Gen. Al Bashir often speaks of *Jihad*. At the 40th anniversary of Sudan's independence, Al Bashir celebrated the spirit of *Jihad* which was engulfing the people of Sudan.

The head of Sudan's ruling party, the *National Islamic Front* (NIF), Dr. Al Turabi, has often declared his goal of an Islamic empire controlling (initially) the horn of Africa (Eritrea, Ethiopia, Somalia, Kenya, Uganda and Sudan). This he calls *"the Grand Islamic Project"*.

At a two week conference of Muslim leaders from 80 countries, hosted by Muammar Gaddafi in Tripoli, Libya (October 1995), strategies to transform Africa into an Islamic continent were discussed. Participants openly admitted that their goals were to make **Arabic** the primary language of the continent and **Islam** the official religion. One SA member of parliament, Farouk Cassim declared: *"It will probably be the*

*To research the Islamic **Jihad** against the Christian Church and to assist persecuted Christians, the author has undertaken extensive mission trips behind the lines.*

biggest revolution to sweep Africa." Head of the Islamic Propagation Centre International (IPCI), Yousuf Deedat, announced afterwards that South Africa was high on the agenda of the Islamic offensive. *"We are going to turn South Africa into a Muslim state. We have the money to do it,"* he said (Sunday Times 22/10/95). At present less than 2 percent of South Africans are Muslims.

What few Westerners understand, however, is that those Muslim leaders who call for the overthrow of all governments and the establishment of an Islamic superstate controlling all aspects of life for every person on earth are not extremists on the fringe of Islam. Actually, *Jihad,* the subjugation and forcible conversion of all people to Islam and world domination are central tenants of Islam. *Jihad* is ranked by many Muslims as **the sixth pillar of Islam.**

Jihad was so important to Muhammad that he declared it to be **the second most important deed in Islam.**

"Allah's apostle was asked, 'What is the best deed?' He replied, 'To believe in Allah and his apostle.' The questioner then asked, 'What is the next (in goodness)?' He replied, 'To participate in Jihad (religious fighting) in Allah's cause.'" – The Hadith, Al Bukhari, Vol. 1 no 25.

Muslims, in fact, divide the world into two sectors: *Dar-al-Islam* (the House of Islam) and *Dar-al-Harb* (The House of War). The only countries considered to be at peace are those where Islamic law (the *Sharia)* is enforced.

Islam in Arabic means submission, surrender or subjugation. A *Muslim* is one who submits. The Arabic word for peace is *Salam. Islam* is the active form of *Salam.* Muslims see themselves as a *"peace making force"* using argument, intrigue, commerce, threats, terrorism, warfare and every other means possible to secure Islam as the only religion worldwide.

Muslims are not permitted to make peace with a non-Muslim country until its inhabitants surrender to Islam. They can agree to a cease fire for a period of time – but never to peace with non-Muslims.

The Quran teaches that Muslims are superior to others: *"Ye (Muslims) are the best of peoples evolved for mankind . . ."* Surah 3:110.

Muslims are forbidden to befriend Jews or Christians: *"O ye who believe! Take not the Jews and the Christians for your friends and protectors. They are but friends and protectors to each other. And he amongst you that turns to them (for friendship) is one of them . . ."* Surah 5:54.

Islam instructs its adherents to fight until their opponents submit. Christians and Jews may be spared if they pay *"Jizya"* – a penalty tax – with willing submission: *"Fight those who believe not in God nor the last day . . . Nor acknowledge the religion of truth, (even if they are) of the people of the Book, until they pay Jizya (tribute taxes) with willing submission, and feel themselves subdued."* Surah 9:29

Derek offers a Gospel booklet to a Muslim in the Nuba Mountains.

"Fight and slay the pagans wherever ye find them and seize them, beleaguer them, and lie in wait (ambush) for them in every strategem (of war); but if they repent and establish regular prayers and practise regular charity, then open the way for them." Surah 9:5 (also 2:193).

For those who resist Islam – execution or mutilation is decreed: *"The punishment of those who wage war against Allah and His apostle, and strive with might and main for mischief through the land is: execution or crucifixion, or the cutting off of the hands and feet from opposite sides or exile from the land . . ."* Surah 5:36.

The *Hadith* which is a record of the words and deeds of Muhammad, is also viewed by Muslims as inspired. Next to the Quran, it is the most important source of Islamic Law. It's teachings are regarded as binding on all Muslims.

The Hadith teaches that apostasy is punishable by death: *"Whoever changes his Islamic religion, kill him."* Vol. 9:57.

A Muslim may not be punished for killing an non-Muslim: *"No Muslim should be killed for killing a kafir (infidel)."* Vol 9:50

Those who die in holy war are guaranteed to go to Heaven. *"The person who participates in Jihad (Holy battles) in Allah's cause and nothing compels him to do so except belief in Allah and His apostle, will be recompensed by Allah either with a reward or booty (if he survives) or will be admitted to paradise (if he is killed)."* Vol 1:35

It may be hard for Christians to understand the concept of such a militant religion, but the primary aim of Islam is not spiritual but political. The ultimate purpose of Islam is the establishment by force of a worldwide Islamic state where *Sharia* law is enforced on all.

To achieve this is the goal of *Jihad.* Islamic scholars identify a multitude of forms that Jihad can take:

1. There is **the Jihad of Words.** Muhammad was a brilliant and gifted orator silencing his enemies in a war of words. In Arab culture it was customary for feuding tribes to select a poet to mock and provoke the opposing forces with spontaneous verses of cursing.

   These linguistic warriors engaged in verbal combat sought to inspire their own side with a sense of superiority and strength whilst undermining the morale of the enemy. This war of words, which

Muslim leaders today such as Gaddaffi, Saddam Hussein and Yassar Arafat still engage in, is actually a war of nerves.

2. There is **the Jihad of Deception.** When Muslims are small in number they can follow the example of Muhammad's 83 followers who fled from persecution in Mecca to Abyssinia (present day Ethiopia). There the Christian *Negus* (king) offered them refuge.

When the Meccans demanded their return as slaves, the Muslim exiles declared that Islam was merely a variation of Christianity. The Muslims selectively recited those passages of the Quran that agreed with the Bible such as the virgin birth and miracles of Jesus and His ascension to Heaven and ultimate return. They remained silent on the unbridgeable differences (such as the denial of the Trinity and the atonement) between the Quran and the Bible.

As a result the Christian Abyssinians protected the Muslims from the Meccans. In this way, when it was most vulnerable, Islam grew and developed in a Christian environment. (If we only demonstrate our Christian love without proclaiming the truth of the Gospel we could strengthen anti-Christian forces).

Muhammad also compromised with the Meccan merchants during a particularly intense time of persecution. Formerly he had fearlessly condemned polytheism. Then, under pressure, he accepted the Meccan belief that Allah had a wife, *Al-lat,* and two daughters, *Al Uzzo* and *Manat* (Surah 53:20-23). Later Muhammad repudiated these so called *Satanic Verses* and claimed that all previous prophets had been tempted by demonic influence.

3. There is **the Jihad of the Sword.** After fleeing to Medina (*the Hijra*) in AD622, Muhammad started to summon his followers to attack and plunder the caravans of Mecca. His followers initially resisted these calls until Muhammad presented a series of *"revelations"* commanding *Jihad* (holy war) and permitting looting (*"Whoever has killed an enemy and has proof of that, will possess his spoils"* – The Hadith, Vol. 4 no. 370).

Where the booty was not large enough, Muhammad held captives as hostages until their families paid a high ransom for their release. Hostage taking has been a common practise in Islam to this day.

This wood and thatch church building in Southern Sudan was considered an important enough target for two helicopter gunships to attack with rockets and burn to the ground.

Those who participate in *Jihad* are granted a blanket absolution (Surah 8:17) and guaranteed to go straight to Paradise (Heaven) if killed.

4. There is the **Jihad of Taxation and Financial Reward.** There who refuse to submit to Islam are forced to pay a special tax for non-Muslims *(Jizya)*. Those who convert to Islam are offered financial rewards or scholarships.

5. There is **the Jihad of Slavery.** Those Muslims who engage in *Jihad* can not only sieze property, extort ransoms and demand taxes, but also capture slaves. The only places in the world today where slavery is still practised are in some Muslim countries.

    In Sudan, the Islamic government uses slavery as an incentive to encourage Arab Northerners to attack the Christian Blacks in the South and as a weapon of terror to destabilize non Muslims. According to the **Sharia,** Muslims are allowed to enslave, own and sell human beings.

6. There is **the Jihad of the *Sharia* Law.** Non-Muslims are degraded to a lower class status and are denied equal access to the law because their testimony is not valid against a Muslim. This even

applies to murder *("No Muslim should be killed for killing an infidel").* The death penalty is applied to anyone who renounces Islam and converts to another religion.

When the wealthy Bedouins of Arabia professed faith in Allah to escape attack, Muhammad did not accept their confession. *("The desert Arabs say 'We believe'. Say, 'Ye have no faith; but ye (only) say 'We have submitted. '"* Surah 49:14) Islam does not place much value on personal faith, but demands surrender to the political rule of the *Sharia.*

It is significant that the calendar of Islam does not begin with the birth of Muhammad, nor the onset of his supposed *"revelation"*, nor the assembling of the first Muslim community, nor the flight of Muslim refugees to Abyssinia. The 12 years of persecution in Mecca were not considered the start of their new religion. The Muslim calendar only begins when Islam became a political state in Medina.

7. There is the **Jihad of Polygamy.** The devastating defeat of the Muslim forces by the Meccans in the battle of Uhud (AD625) led to what could be considered one of Islam's greatest victories. So many of his men were killed that Muhammad permitted his men to take up to 4 wives (Surah 4:3, 4).

With the advent of Western medicine, infant mortality has plummeted. And the Muslim birthrate has skyrocketed. Muslims are increasing in number twice as fast as other religions. This is due to birth control and abortion in Western lands and polygamy in Muslim lands. Muslims are not increasing much by missionary outreaches, but by having many children. Polygamy has become one of Islam's most effective

*A Nuba man whose feet have been cut off by the NIF in the name of **Sharia** law.*

187

weapons for Holy War, providing Islam with a disproportionate numerical advantage.

8. There is **the Jihad of the Spirits.** According to the Quran, Muslims are not only men and women but also spirits who fight for the spread of Islam (Surah 46:29-33 and 72:1-15). A Muslim is to fight on Muhammad's behalf both in his life and after his death (Hadith Vol. 1 chapter 43).

Clearly Islam is a religion of force which denies basic freedom. No Muslim even has the freedom to change or leave his religion. The huge block of over 1 billion Muslims presents **the greatest political and military threat to the Western world and the greatest missionary challenge to the Christian Church.** Muslim states are the most severe persecutors of Christians, and Muslim terrorist groups are the most vicious hijackers, kidnappers, bombers and assassins. Islam is a challenge that we cannot ignore.

How we chose to respond, in prayer, publications, proclamation, projects and persistent vigilance will determine much of the course of history in the coming 21st century.

The statue of General Charles Gordon in Khartoum – before it was torn down by Muslim extremists.

"The desert tribes will bow before Him and His enemies will lick the dust . . . All kings will bow down to Him and all nations will serve Him." Psalm 72:11

25

UNDER SIEGE IN THE NUBA

It was hot. Extremely hot. Already 45° Celcius (110°F) in the shade and we weren't in the shade! The palm trees and occasional camels reminded me that we were in North Africa – at the Southernmost edge of the vast Sahara Desert. The steep rocky mountain slopes that we had repeatedly traversed are part of the Nuba Mountains of Central Sudan. Our GPS (Global Positioning System) confirmed that we were inside the famed *10-40 Window* – at 11° latitude in fact.

Appointment with an Ambush

I was somewhat delirious and dehydrated from heat exhaustion, but I knew we were out of both food and water. Just to move was agony. My every muscle ached (even ones that I didn't know I had). That wasn't too surprising – just in the past three days we had walked over 100 km up and down precarious paths over dozens of mountains and across a great open plain – between enemy garrisons.

The Frontline team walked over 180 kms across the Nuba Mountains to deliver 4 tonnes of Bibles and relief aid.

Most of the villages in the Nuba Mountains have been destroyed.

The previous day we had started out at 3 a.m. and climbed silently up and down steep mountains and walked for 12 hours. Then we had delivered Bibles, books, agricultural tools and seed to a village and showed the *"Jesus"* film in Arabic to the entire community.

We had barely fallen asleep when my alarm sounded at 2 a.m. and we started out on a five hour climb and hike to an airstrip. Unknown to us the radio message we were responding to was false. Our evacuation flight had not been diverted to this remote airstrip. Instead, Arab soldiers of the National Islamic Front (NIF) government of Sudan were heading to that same airstrip to ambush us.

It had already been a stunning mission trip of great extremes. Extreme terrain. Oppressive heat, unrelenting, mind numbing heat. Yet some nights were quite cold. There had been vast distances to be covered – first by air over 3 hours into Central Sudan, far behind enemy lines. Then many hours and days of walking up and down the jagged Nuba Mountains.

The needs we confronted were desperate. Many people were hungry, some starving. The NIF government of Sudan (GOS) has declared *Jihad* (holy war) and is waging a cruel and relentless scorched earth campaign against the Nuba people. Most of the Nuba villages have been looted and destroyed. Most of their crops have been burned. Most

190

of their livestock has been stolen. Even wells have been poisoned in what the GOS calls *"Tamsit"* (combing). As one GOS official so ruthlessly put it: *"We're draining the sea to catch the fish!"* Everything necessary to sustain life is a target to be destroyed by the GOS forces.

Most of the Nubans are dressed in threadbare clothes or tattered rags. Many are completely naked. They have fled up the mountains to escape from the fertile plains which are now dominated and devastated by the marauding GOS forces.

Rock of Ages

The Nuba Mountains cover an area of 50 000 square kilometres. Some of the mountains rise to 1 500 metres above sea level. These mountains are natural fortresses with very steep slopes. A handful of men in key positions can (and do) easily protect the precarious paths that wind precipitously up through the rocks.

Life, and travel, in these mountainous sanctuaries is extremely harsh. The heat is merciless. The terrain is severe – rocky, steep and thorn bush covered. Every day the women have to walk up to six hours away from their village in order to collect water. They then balance the containers on their heads for the long, careful, steep ascent back to their village.

Slavery is still practised in Sudan as an incentive to encourage Arab Northerners to attack Christian blacks..

Over 10 000 Bibles and Christian books were delivered to the beleaguered Christians in the Nuba Mountains.

Most Nubans are barefoot. The fortunate ones have some sandals. Shoes are rare.

The Nubans are Black people who speak Arabic. They are geographically and culturally a frontier between the Arab North and the Black South. After the collapse of the Ancient Christian kingdoms of Nubia, Alwa and Dotawo, and the Islamic invasion of the North of Sudan around the 15th Century, many of the survivors took refuge in the Nuba Mountains. Then, over the centuries, escaped slaves from the human cargo of Arab caravans en route from the heart of Africa to the Muslim world fled to the Nuba Mountains for refuge.

The architecture of homes in the Nuba reflect this diversity of origins. Some homes are built of dry stone reminiscent of the Zimbabwe Ruins, others of clay with circular doors similar to those found amongst the Dogon in Mali. There are more than 50 distinct ethnic groups in the Nuba.

Islamic *Jihad*

The official government policy of Islamisation (carried on since 1922) has succeeded in persuading 40% of the Nuba to become (at least nominally) Muslim. But even these Nuban Muslims are united with the Christian majority in opposing the NIF government in Khartoum.

Most of the Nuba churches have been destroyed. About one million Nubans have been forced into concentration camps.

In these camps children are separated from their parents and family and are indoctrinated into the fundamentalist brand of Islam adhered to by the NIF government. Later these children will be brain washed to wage *Jihad* against their own people. Nuba women have been methodically raped in these camps so that the next generation will be more Arab than Nuba.

About 400 000 Nubans are holding out in the liberated areas controlled by the Sudanese Peoples Liberation Army (SPLA) resistance movement. These Arabic speaking Nuba people are an island of Christianity in a sea of Islam. These brave and resilient people have steadfastly resisted all attempts to subjugate or annihilate them.

Behind Enemy Lines

That is why we had travelled over 7 000 km from Cape Town, in South Africa, to help these desperately needy and courageous people. Our

It took 250 volunteers to carry the four tonnes of Bibles, books, seed and agricultural tools.

193

charter aircraft had flown in 4 metric tonnes of Bibles, books, Gospel booklets, educational materials, agricultural tools and vegetable seed.

As we had landed on the dry, dusty airstrip I could see armed men walking through the cloud of dust towards us. I fervently prayed that these were SPLA soldiers and not GOS troops! The intense Nuban heat hit me as I opened the aircraft door and climbed out to greet the soldiers. They welcomed us warmly. The officer in charge quickly organised a work party to off-load our aircraft.

The pilot was somewhat impatient to take off as quickly as possible. *"This airstrip is within artillery range of the nearby GOS garrison. They've mortared this airstrip before"*, he explained.

As we watched our charter aircraft take off we felt something like Cortes must have felt after burning his ships! We were far behind enemy lines in the midst of the longest war of this century.

Steve pointed out to me where he and Scott had run for cover when the GOS helicopter gunships had attacked the mission team last year. They had no sooner landed and off-loaded the Bibles and relief aid when two MI-24 Hind helicopter gunships came roaring over this very same landing strip – pouring machine cannon fire and rockets directly into the midst of the crowd that had assembled to receive the aid. The gunships circled and made repeated strafing runs over the area. They systematically rocketed and shot wherever people were fleeing.

The team saw two Nuba women shredded by machine cannon fire. Missiles were fired. Huge bolders were blown to pieces. The ground was churned up by the machine gun fire as Steve sprinted for cover. Our men ran through a gauntlet of schrapnel and bullets and escaped up the mountain to a secure area controlled by the resistance movement. *"You're the first visitors we've ever had in this area. Nobody has ever brought us any aid before,"* they were told.

When Steve and Scott returned to the Nuba Mountains later that year, with over 5 000 Bibles and books, the local Christians were very surprised and greatly encouraged. *"We thought you'd never come back, you have encouraged us with your return,"* declared one church leader.

Body, Mind and Spirit

There was even more excitement this time as they saw Steve return yet again – with more people and many more Bibles, books (over 10 000 Gospel booklets, books and Bibles – mostly in Arabic) and relief aid.

They recognised that the materials we had brought represented the sacrifices, love and prayers of hundreds of others from around the world. To know that they are not alone, that they're not forgotten is a great encouragement to these long suffering people. It was also clear that they appreciated the commitment of Frontline Fellowship to keep coming back.

Our ministry strategy in the Nuba is to minister to body, mind and spirit. For this reason we transported in and distributed: one tonne of vegetable seed, farming tools (hundreds of axes, hoes and machetes) and 100 water containers (20 litre jerry cans) – for the desperate physical needs; one tonne of school materials, school textbooks, exercise books, charts, blackboards and chalk – for the educational needs; and two tonnes of Bibles (1 400 full Bibles in Arabic), Christian books (over 2 000) and Gospel booklets (over 7 000), as well as Gospel Recordings *Messengers,* and the *Jesus* film in Arabic – for the spiritual needs.

Almost every day we walked to a different village. My brother, Derek, who co-ordinates our *Love in Action* ministry, personally distributed the agricultural tools, seed and other relief items to the leaders of 11 different congregations. I would bring greetings, proclaim the Gospel and entrust a library of books and a box of Gospel Literature to

Derek personally distributed 2 tonnes of educational and agricultural materials to 11 congregations.

195

the local pastor. Steve would then present Bible stories to the people using the Gospel Recordings *Messengers* (tough tape recorders that can be solar powered or hand wound) with flip charts. These audio visual presentations always drew large crowds and held the people riveted as they heard the Bible message in Arabic and saw it illustrated in dramatic colourful illustrations.

As on previous trips, Steve entrusted these tape recorders, each with a full set of nine audio cassettes and flip charts (about 9 hours of Bibles stories with accompanying pictures), to trusted evangelists and pastors in remote areas.

Getting There Before Hollywood

Then, each night when the sun set, we would rig up a large canvas screen, crank up the generator and show the *Jesus* film in Arabic with the 16 mm projector. Many hundreds, sometimes thousands, of soldiers and civilians would come to see this two hour Gospel film. For the vast majority of the people it was the first time they had ever seen any film. (It is always good to get there before Hollywood – with the Gospel!)

The Nuba people certainly could relate to the *Jesus* film better than most of us could. They are a rural people dependent on farming and livestock for survival, whose only form of transportation is by foot. And

*Almost every night the Frontline team screened the **Jesus** film (in Arabic) to a different village. For thousands of Nubans this was the first time that they had ever seen any film.*

under Islamic *Sharia* law, Christians are flogged and crucified in the Nuba Mountains. (GOS troops have even used live crucified Christians as target practise.)

Some may question the value of using films for evangelism. We warn the people that what we are about to show them is only a film with actors. Nobody knows what Jesus actually looked like – nor do we need to – it is what He taught and did that is important. And every word in

Steve has presented the Gospel Recordings audio visual presentations in dozens of villages in the Nuba.

the film is from the Gospel of Luke.

It is impossible for us to appreciate the enormous impact that audio visual presentations of the Gospel have – especially on rural people in remote areas. This made the logistical challenge of carrying a 16 mm projector and generator up and down innumerable mountains in scorching heat well worthwhile.

There were nights when it seemed impossible to screen the film – in rain, shielding the projector during a dust storm, with the sound of heavy weapons in the background, with Arab forces flares lighting up the night. Yet we managed to screen the Jesus film in eight different areas of the Nuba Mountains.

In a war zone like the Nuba Mountains of Sudan, every trip is dangerous. Every day has its risks. A foreigner attracts intense interest and the GOS offers great rewards for any information on foreign visitors. Therefore, we have to keep moving to different villages under serious time constraints. How then can we clearly communicate as much of the Gospel and discipleship principles to these suffering rural people in a language they understand, in as short a time as possible?

We have found that a combination of Gospel Recordings Bible stories and the *Jesus* film in Arabic are very effective communication tools. After these audio visual presentations we preach the Gospel, distribute Gospel literature and entrust a library of discipleship books to the local church.

The Gospel vs Jihad

Over the last 10 years the Nubans have endured a cruel and relentless scorched earth campaign. Bibles have been illegal. Missionaries have been banned. All flights, even relief aid flights, have been forbidden. All contact with the outside world has been cut off. The Nubans have been isolated, persecuted and targeted for destruction. Yet these brave and beleaguered people have

Hope for Sudan: a Father reads the Ten Commandments with his child.

steadfastly refused to give up. They continue to survive and persevere – to fight for their Faith and for freedom. Yet they felt so alone. A hidden people fighting a forgotten war for survival.

By our threefold ministries of Love in Action, Literature distribution and Leadership training we are strengthening the believers in Sudan to not only survive the severe persecution, but also to win their persecutors to Christ. We had the great joy of seeing even people from a Muslim background committing themselves to Christ during this mission trip.

Mutilations and Landmines

The harshness of the National Islamic Front (NIF) government of Sudan was very evident. We walked over the scorched earth, passed burned out homes and fields. We met people who had been mutilated by the Arab government forces. Under *Sharia* law amputation of limbs is decreed for various offences. We spoke with amputees who had had arms or feet cut off by the Muslims.

One man, James Krma, a 52 year old father of 5 children, and an Episcopal church member, related to me how the NIF soldiers had come

198

and destroyed his village, Adudu, on 26 February 1997. The Arabs had accused him of supporting *"the rebels"* and after a week of fruitless interrogation they cut off his arm at the elbow.

Many others have lost limbs to landmines. As we were loading our charter aircraft in preparation to fly into the Nuba, two Nubans who had lost feet to landmines and had now recovered asked if we would please take them with us. Although they had lost limbs they were cheerful and delighted to be able to fly back home – even though we were flying back to a war zone. Our aircraft risked being shot down as it violated the GOS flight ban and once safely landed these amputees would need to negotiate mountains on crutches. They would also face, once again, the real dangers of landmines, slave raids and aerial bombardments. Nevertheless, they were eager to go *"home"* to the Nuba Mountains!

On landing in the Nuba we were asked if six wounded Nubans (most from landmines) could be evacuated by our charter aircraft. We were glad to see them airlifted to safety and medical treatment at the hospital in Kenya, yet it was sobering to be so forcibly reminded that we were about to walk many hours in an area where landmines (the devil's seed) had been sown.

The Frontline team conducted 65 meetings in the Nuba Mountains during this trip.

Then there was the real possibility of an ambush or air attack.

We often heard Antonov bombers or GOS reconnaissance aircraft in the distance. Our eyes continually scanned the skies, the horizons and the bushes for any signs of danger. The intense concentration of anticipating an attack, realising that each step could be our last, makes one thoughtful and prayerful. From the tops of some mountains we were shown the Arab government garrisons. On some of our night hikes strict silence had to be maintained as we walked between enemy garrisons on the plain.

*A Nuban man whose arm had been cut off by the NIF because of **Sharia** law.*

Record Breaking Column

During our outreach to the Nuba Mountains we walked about 180 km with 16 mm film projector, generator, fuel and film, with boxes of Gospel literature, up and down the steep mountain slopes. Our initial column of volunteers to carry the four tonnes of Bibles, Gospel literature, 16 mm projector, reels, generator, fuel, books, seed and agricultural tools up the mountain was over 250 strong – including porters/carriers and military escorts.

It was an impressive sight seeing the long column of people briskly moving up the steep mountain slopes, snaking through the mountain valleys, cheerfully carrying the four tonnes of Bibles, books and relief aid. Most of the carriers were women. They explained that the men were away in the army, fighting the Arabs. Yet it seemed that in their culture the women normally carried the heavy loads!

According to one history book, the longest human column was the *Safari* of ex-US President Theodore Roosevelt in Kenya in 1909. His column consisted of 100 porters, with an average of 60 pounds to carry.

Our column consisted of 200 carriers and 50 soldiers (escorts). The average load carried was 25 kg (almost 60 pounds).

Mountain Marathons

At one point of the steep ascent whilst sweating profusely, I noticed the one legged Nuban woman (whom we had transported in on the aircraft) hop past me on her crutches! I was shocked – and inspired to step up my pace accordingly! The harsh terrain and vicious scorched earth campaign being waged against them, combined with their tenacious faith, have made the Nubans incredibly tough.

At one point Derek exclaimed: *"I run, swim or go to the gym virtually every day of the week. I have run the Comrades and Two Oceans Marathons. How is it possible that these people can leave me in the dust?"* Although I do not maintain the same level of fitness as my brother, I felt similarly impressed by our Nuban friends *"mountain goat"* fitness. Steve had represented South Africa in long distance hikes and speed marches in the Swiss Alps. He did a lot better, but also had to push himself to keep up with their cracking pace. A lifetime of walking in the Nuba Mountains gave our hosts a natural advantage!

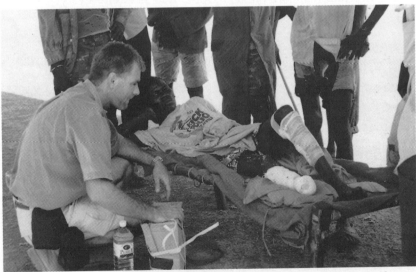

Several Nubans, including this man who had lost his foot to a landmine explosion, were flown out for emergency medical treatment.

Each day I forced my body to climb and walk faster. Ignoring blisters on my feet, aching muscles and the chaffing that seemed to rub the insides of my thighs raw, I pushed on. On one particular day I was up with the advance party of military escorts maintaining their pace for several hours. It was gratifying at the top of one of the highest mountains to have some of them compliment my efforts. *"You are very strong, very fast, strong like a Nuba!"* declared one.

I felt half dead at the time, but that encouragement inspired me to keep on keeping on! On another memorable occasion I was informed that we had walked in 12 hours what another team had taken three days to cover.

"Everyone can be a Missionary"

During those long, hot days of walking I thought often of an article in a popular Christian magazine that I had read just prior to the trip. It was entitled *"Everyone Can Be A Missionary!"* Under the circumstances the title seemed more than incongruous.

Of course, I believe every Christian should be missionary minded and prayerfully support mission work. And naturally every Christian

The Frontline team sometimes had to walk for 12 hours in a day, often in 45° heat.

202

should be a witness to others. However, the tasks and calling of a missionary demands total life long commitment, dedication in training and perseverance in service.

Can everyone be a doctor, an engineer, a pilot, or a mother? It seemed to me that the article had devalued the calling of a missionary. The writer of the article had apparently based her amazing conclusion that *"everyone can be a missionary"* on her two week mission trip to Malawi.

Well, I have received first aid training and have administered first aid to injured people – but I would never call myself a doctor or a nurse! Everyone should learn how to handle basic first aid in an emergency, but we are fooling ourselves if we confuse what we dabble in, almost as a hobby, with the specialised training, experience and responsibilities of a career professional. This is the same in missions. Cross cultural communication and church planting amongst Animists or Muslims is extremely difficult and requires thorough preparation and a life time commitment.

The technological advantages our generation has over previous generations of missionaries is astounding. It took David Livingstone many weeks by boat and over four months by ox-cart to reach his first mission station at Kuruman. It took him years to walk across Africa – journeys that we can now complete in hours by air and days by four wheel drive vehicles. However, while it is infinitely easier to reach the mission fields today – it is also all too easy to leave.

This modern mobility is therefore both a blessing and a curse. Fast, easy travel has also led to the whole problem of superficiality and shallowness in missions. The hectic schedules and packed programmes of short termers cannot measure up to the impact of a dedicated career missionary couple settling amongst an unreached people and investing their lives in discipling a community.

Have we sacrificed quality for quantity? Are we replacing Reformation and revival with relief aid? We have not been called to make converts, but disciples. Patrick Johnstone's conclusion is that we should only invest in short term mission workers when they are being used in an ongoing ministry for long term goals.

So, can anybody be a missionary? No, most people aren't even Christians.

Can every Christian be a missionary? No, because many Christians are selfish, hyper-sensitive to criticism and unwilling to suffer discomfort, let alone danger and diseases. All Christians are called to be faithful witnesses evangelising their neighbours and colleagues at work. All Christians are called to support missions – but each of us have different life callings and responsibilities.

The "Glamour" of Missions

Another phrase that was discussed at length by our mission team in the Nuba was *"the glamour of missions."* Some people express the view that missionary work is glamourous! As you can imagine, this became the brunt of many a joke in the Nuba Mountains.

Glamourous? Missions is exciting, yes! Challenging, definitely! Glamorous – hardly ever! Yes, we do sometimes have singing choirs welcoming us to remote villages, and large crowds at services. But, inbetween there is sweltering heat, dust storms, flies, dysentry, boils, sunburn, backache, blisters and malaria.

There is seldom any privacy as the children in particular find strange foreigners like ourselves fascinating. They crowd around, touching, pulling, examining and peeping at every opportunity. Nights are mostly sleepless – either because of mosquitos and other flying, crawling and biting insects or because of the disturbing noises, particularly gunfire, but also dogs barking and roosters crowing (sometimes from as early as 2:30 a.m.) – right in our huts!

Then we could mention howling dust storms, dust in our hair, ears, eyes, nose, mouth, in fact in everything – including the 16 mm projector causing endless jams! The micro organisms in the water are too small to see with the unaided eye, but they can certainly cause great discomfort, pain and sickness. In Sudan every drop of water we cook our food in or drink needs to be filtered and boiled. However, it would be rude not to accept any food or water offered by any local host. Inevitably, on every field trip, we end up sick with some form of dysentry, or worse. What we pray never to suffer from is the life long diseases caused by guinea worm or *"river blindness."*

*Literally thousands made public commitments to Christ after the **Jesus** film and GR presentations.*

Some of the other *"glamorous"* aspects of missions which we experienced on this trip included: walking all day to an empty church only to find that the organiser hadn't organised anything; sleeping amidst the goats in a corral covered in cow dung and goat droppings; and being put up in a cave where all the men crowded in to have a meal in our *"bedroom"* – spitting bones onto our floor and packs while dogs and chickens raced in to pick up the scraps of food littered over our sleeping area!

One night we were plagued by rats. They scurried all over the walls, roof, floor, and our packs. (My one canvas bag still has all the holes made by the rats as they sought to reach our food). Steve and I batted them away with machetes. Yet they still came on. When we finally went to sleep it was with a machete in one hand and a flashlight in the other. As Steve warded off rats climbing onto his bed, I quipped: *"While you've got your hands full – with the machete and flashlight – do be careful of swatting any mosquitos that land on your nose!"*

On another occasion, Derek and I were caught up in a chaotic riot when we attempted to distribute Gospel tracts in a market place. The people literally fought to obtain a tract.

Time and space preclude me from describing all the problems caused by cross cultural confusion, miscommunications, deceptions, thefts, bureaucratic obstructionism and other man made disasters.

Maintaining a Sense of Humour

Of course it is essential to maintain a good sense of humour in the field. The Nuba Christians do. James whose one arm had been amputated by the Arabs, picked up one of our machetes from the selection of farm tools I offered him. With a glint in his eyes he exclaimed: *"Jalabas!"* (the nickname for the Arabs). Another man who had lost his leg smiled as he extended his right arm and his fore finger: *"At least I still have my trigger finger!"*

It was a mission trip of extremes. Extreme heat, extreme exertion and extremely good opportunities for ministry. Many thousands made public commitments to Christ in response to our 63 evangelistic and teaching messages in the Nuba.

Now we were walking in the dark to a remote airstrip for our evacuation flight. *"We're very close now!"* said our guide. Yes, they'd said that several times in the last few hours. I mentally checked through the list of *"gems"*:

"It never rains this time of the year" (That night our open air film showing was washed out in a rain storm).

"The Arabs never operate at night and they never try to come up on the mountains." (That night we were woken up by heavy gunfire close by as the SPLA fought off an attempt by the Arabs to come up the mountain. Several days later an Arab attack at the same location killed several people.

"It's okay to drink. The water is safe." (I got terribly sick from that one cup of water).

"It never gets cold in the Nuba." (In fact, we did get very cold on a couple of wind blown nights, but I had left my sleeping bag behind to save weight)!

"It cannot get worse" (Yet day by day, conditions did deteriorate into ever greater challenges!)

Evading The Enemy

A breathless soldier startled me out of my thoughts *"Security alert!"* he shouted. *"The aircraft is not going to this airstrip!"* It turned out that we'd woken up at at 2 a.m. and hiked five hours to this location in vain. The radio message we had received at 10 p.m. the previous night had been false. At that very moment GOS forces were moving into the area.

Only by God's grace did we escape an ambush laid by the GOS at the airstrip.

That night our military escort laid ambush positions around our camp. We knew that the GOS forces were nearby. Our kit was packed. We slept fitfully, waking at every sound. We were ready to sling our backpacks and run at a moment's notice. Suddenly at midnight we were awoken by furious bursts of machine gun fire – very close by. We scrambled for our kit and prepared to move.

"Everything is under control – you can rest," the leader assured us. However, he related to us news of a build up of enemy forces not too far away threatening the village where we had ministered and showed the *Jesus* film the previous night. *"That could also threaten the other airstrip!"* It was pointed out that our evacuation flight could be in danger.

We prayed. I realised that it was my 9th wedding anniversary (and the 3rd consecutive one I'd spent in Sudan far away from Lenora). It was hard to know how to celebrate it as even water was scarce.

Walking to ministry gives one energy. Walking to nowhere because of human error or maliciousness makes your feet feel as heavy as lead. Yet we used our delay to show the *Jesus* film to another village. Fortunately we had just enough fuel for the generator for one more showing!

Yet another 3 a.m. start to the next day walking to another airstrip rendezvous. Once there we checked the airstrip and a soldier walked over the landing area with a mine sweeper. It was a tense wait, but a couple of hours later our aircraft came roaring in at tree top level and made a bumpy landing. Goodbyes were said and we gave some of our waterbottles and kit to our escorts.

Then we were racing down the strip and hurtling into the sky. After so many days of walking it seemed incredible to suddenly cover so much distance so quickly. My mind was racing faster than the aircraft as I pulled out my writing pad and began to plan the follow up projects to this our thirtieth mission trip into Sudan.

Prayer, Praise and Planning

We praised God for the 16th anniversary of Frontline Fellowship. The Lord has

The Scripture commands us to care for widows and orphans.

wonderfully guided, provided for and protected our missionaries in so many dangerous and difficult areas for nearly 17 years. Just in the previous 3 years, in Sudan alone, Frontline Fellowship had delivered over 90 000 Bibles and Christian books in 21 languages, to 11 different regions. We have also conducted over 1 000 meetings inside Sudan, including: four *Pastors Training Courses,* three *Medical Workshops,* a *Biblical Worldview Seminar* for Secondary School Teachers, a *God and Government Seminar* for civil leaders and a *Reformation and Revival Seminar* for chaplains. We had also restored or established three clinics, delivered tonnes of medicines and delivered an ambulance.

But so much more still needed to be done.

26

SPEAKING UP FOR THE SOUTH

The virtual news blackout over Sudan is very disturbing. Sudan is the largest country in Africa. It has the **longest war of this century** still raging (since 1955). The South Sudanese people are the **oldest Christian community in Africa.** There has been a strong Christian presence in South Sudan since the Third Century AD. Sudan is the site of **the most vicious anti-Christian persecution** raging anywhere in the world today. Hundreds of Christian villages have been razed to the ground. Over 1½ million Christians have been murdered or starved to death by a man-made famine.

Hundreds of Christian men have been crucified. Tens of thousands of Christian young people have been sold into slavery. Christians are enduring inhumane torture. It is no exaggeration to call what is happening in Sudan, genocide. The Christians in Sudan are literally on the frontline of the battle for Faith and freedom. Yet, how seldom do we ever read or hear anything of their plight? The church in Sudan is experiencing real revival and spectacular growth. More Muslims are coming to Christ in Sudan than almost anywhere else in the world.

It is our deep concern to see the Christian publications of the West publicising the plight of our beleaguered brethren and mobilising the prayer, pressure and support so desperately

A Nuban herdsman risks his life by leaving the mountains to provide grazing for his cattle on the vast plains below.

needed. Help us to make known the plight of Southern Sudan. Write letters to your local newspapers, write to your elected representative, urge that diplomatic and economic pressure be brought to bear upon the Government of Sudan to stop their atrocities. Encourage your local radio stations to report on the incredible testimonies of suffering and Christian courage in Sudan. Ensure that Sudan is regularly remembered in prayer at your church.

Take this book, purchase more copies or photocopy excerpts and post them to your local Christian editors. Write letters to the press urging more coverage on the untold stories of Christian courage amidst severe persecution in Sudan.

When speaking up for the Christians in Sudan I have often received these reactions: *"Why are the Christians fighting back against the Muslims? Surely they should just turn the other cheek?"* and *"Why don't the Christians just pray? They can win Muslims to Christ by love – not by war."*

The simple answers to these concerns are that the Christians in Sudan are praying. They pray long, hard and deep. Their prayer meetings make ours seem juvenile. There's nothing like facing violent death, sudden bombardments and man-made famine to deepen anyone's prayer life!

Their evangelistic zeal should also be obvious. More Muslims are coming to Christ in Sudan than anywhere else in the world. Twenty years ago the Christians made up 5% of the total population. Today Christians comprise over 20% of Sudan (and 80% of Southern Sudan).

Perhaps if our food supplies had been pillaged or destroyed, our churches had been razed to the ground, our relatives crucified and our sons captured

Steve with some young Nubans.

Sudanese Christians rejoice to receive the Word of God.

by slave raiders – then we would be fighting to protect our wives and children as well.

> *"Do not be afraid of them. Remember the Lord great and awesome, and fight for your brethren, your sons, your daughters, your wives, and your houses."*   *Nehemiah 4:14*

The opportunities for ministry in Southern Sudan are so great. The suffering is so intense. The needs are so desperate. The largest country in Africa, in the grip of the longest war of this century, requires our greatest missionary efforts. The oldest community of Christians in Africa, suffering the most severe persecution in the world demands our most urgent and wholehearted assistance. Frontline Fellowship needs your help to rise to this challenge:

Please join with us in fervent prayer that the sufferings of our Christian brethren in Sudan become known to the whole world, that the persecutors be exposed and opposed, that peace – with justice – be firmly established.

"Assuredly, I say to you, inasmuch as you did it to one of the least of these My brethren, you did it to Me."   *Matthew 25:40*

211

APPENDIX

A MESSAGE FROM SUDAN

"Tell our brothers and sisters that the people here are still full of hope and that there are still smiles on the faces of the children, in spite of their suffering, in spite of persecution, in spite of constant fear of attack. Those smiles put us to shame. I believe that after their suffering, justice and peace will come. They tell us that they feel forgotten by the world; that even the church seems to forget them. There are many other places in Sudan where people have no water, no clothes, food, school, or the basic essentials for survival.

*The church has tried to tell people that we care and pray for you. But if we love, prayer alone is not sufficient. Of course, Christ told us to pray, but **prayer must lead to action;** prayer without action is empty. As St Paul said, 'Faith without action is dead.' It is the same with prayer. The people here need peace and justice. Enough is enough. The world feels that Sudan is not a priority on its agenda. But it will be impossible to achieve a better world without peace in Sudan. The threat of fundamentalist Islam will spread beyond these borders.*

I have nothing against Muslims; we love all. Love goes beyond race, colour, creed. But we must say that what is happening to us is perpetrated by Islamic fundamentalism, which is determined to destroy our religion, our culture, our language, our roots.

*Dear brothers and sisters, there can be no one-way dialogue. Dialogue requires mutual acceptance and respect. We are open for this – not for political or commercial gain. We want to live in peace. But we are suffering so much. We want to tell our brothers and sisters abroad that **we are suffering a genocide in our country,** especially in the Nuba Mountains. **Slavery is a reality** – now. Men and women are taken and sold as slaves. The Government of Sudan denies this, but we have witnesses and evidence of names and places.*

What does the world expect from us? This is a holy war – a jihad, with hatred in those who attack us. Listen to their words . . . they say they are going to kill us 'infidels' . . . my people are called 'infidels'.

212

They use food to Islamicise and Arabise us and they destroy Christians and Africans with terror and torture.

Ghost houses are a reality and it is a pity that those who visit Northern Sudan say they have not 'seen' ghost houses. Do they expect the regime to show them?

*Dear brothers and sisters, **be our voice.** We are hungry, persecuted, naked, with no schools. But we are dignified. We have maintained our dignity and we live full of hope that the day of liberation will come.*

*You cannot live in isolation. No man is an island. You cannot expect us to **live in peace if you allow arms to the Government of Sudan** to kill our people. Africa does not need bombs or mines; Africa needs education, development, justice . . . these will lead to peace. Stops arms coming to the regime in Khartoum: **stop the bombs and the fuel** which makes it possible for them to move their tanks. Create safe corridors, so food can reach hungry children; create safe havens for peace. We have great hope – in God first – and also in you.*

*To the media I say: **rather than printing scandals of famous people on your front pages, print the suffering and dignity of the Sudanese people.** The media should continue to apply pressure on politicians to encourage them to realise that it is a noble cause to help and to serve humanity.*

May God bless you.   *Bishop Macram*

Renewed fighting always leads to great social upheavals as whole communities flee.

A CRY FOR HELP

"The centre of Islamic fundamentalism is in the Sudan, from where it extends into Africa. The Islamic fundamentalists say: ' The Christian era is ended, and the year 2 000 is the beginning of the Islamic era'. The Arab-Islamic penetration in Sudan is seen by us Africans in Sudan not as a spiritual development, but as 'conquest' and complete colonisation, aiming at a total assimilation, using every means of war, terror, torture and famine. The Black African race in Sudan is threatened. An Arab minority in the Sudan wants to assimilate the Africans to destroy African traditions, beliefs and way of life. And to do this by force. The Arab language has been imposed on the Africans against their will as a vehicle of Islamization and of creating an Islamic State. The struggling people of Sudan have been suffering not thirty- eight years, but over a century with no-one to liberate them. We count on your prayers and your support in helping us to have true freedom and peace with justice."

Bishop Paride Taban

Bishop Paride Taban ministring among the Kacipo people in Boma.

A CHAPLAIN'S REQUEST

It seems that the outside world is ignorant about the suffering and persecution of Christians in South Sudan by the Islamic government in Khartoum. If this is the punishment of Sudan mentioned in Isaiah 18:1-6 then everything has happened as written in those verses. It is also true that the Sudanese are raising their hands to God in prayer (Psalm 68:31).

The persecution has forced many Sudanese Christians to have a strong faith in the power of God.

Within the (SPLA) army chaplains have been appointed. Prayers are being conducted on the Parade grounds and before any military activities are begun.

I appeal to all Christians around the world to pray for the work of the Chaplaincy so that all the SPLA soldiers may be strong – both spiritually and physically in the field.

Rev. Justin; Rev. John; Rev. Peter; Rev. Moses; Rev. David

215

AN APPEAL FOR HELP

The war between the Christians and Muslims of Sudan has resulted in the destruction of most social and economic infrastructures, the collapse of education and health services. The children are growing wild without proper education. The rate of mortality is very high due to the lack of proper health services.

The war is not a civil nor a political war, it is religious war between Christians and Muslims. Christians are resisting what, in effect, is genocide, arabization and Islamization. The Muslims are determined to impose the Islamic religion upon the Christians and to turn Sudan into an Arabic state. This cause has been supported by Islamic countries like Iran.

As most of you should have been hearing over the media, Sudan has become the centre to train terrorists, it has been now included on the list of terrorist supporting countries. Those who want to know more about the Sudan let them turn to the Biblical verses: Ps. 87:4, Numbers 12:1, Isaiah 18 talks about the suffering people of the Sudan – to mention a few.

For the cause of our Faith in Christ we have been persecuted. Many have been killed, tortured and even starved to death. Despite all these atrocities we as Christians do stand firm in our Faith, knowing that Jesus Christ honours faithfulness and is fighting with us.

I am therefore appealing to the outside world to pay attention to what is going on in Sudan: Christians, Brothers and Sisters, please do come and rescue your brothers and sisters from the mouth of the lion, before we are finished. The slogan of the Islamicists is "we want only the land not the people". They termed us as infidels – but we love God.

With Thanks,

Rev. Kenneth Baringwa,
Bishop's Commissar,
Diocese of Mundri
Episcopal Church
New Sudan

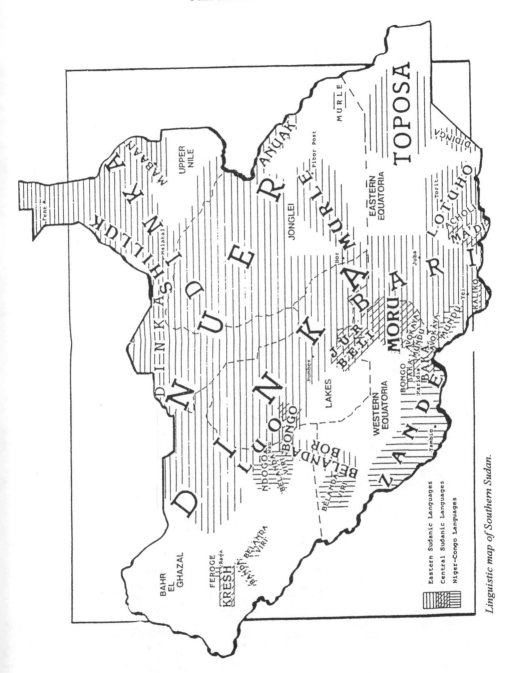

Linguistic map of Southern Sudan.

States of Sudan

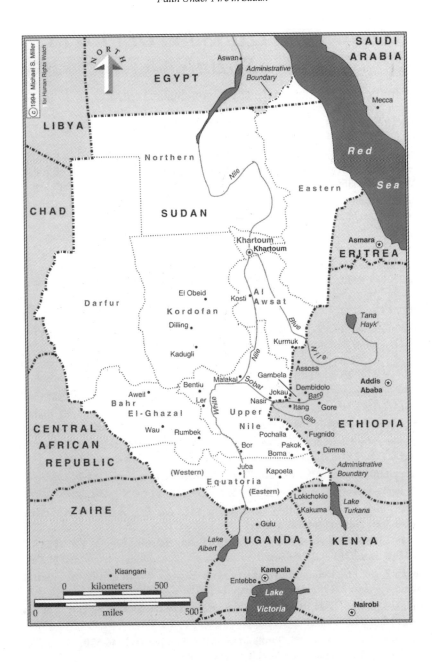

ORGANISATIONS INVOLVED IN SUDAN

For further information on the situation in Sudan contact:

African Rights (AR) – 11 Marshalsea Road, London SE1 1EP, England. Tel: (171) 717-1224. Fax: (171) 717 1240.

Association of Christian Resource Organisations Serving Sudan (ACROSS) – Studio House, Argwings Kodhek Rd, PO Box 21033, Nairobi, Kenya. Tel: (254-2) 723-680/569-685/569-688. Fax: (254 -2) 72-6509. E-Mail: Across @ maf. org.

Christian Solidarity International (CSI) – PO Box 70, Zelglistr. 64, CH-8122 Binz, Switzerland. Tel: (41-1) 980-4700. Fax: (41-1) 980-4715.

Episcopal Church of The Sudan (ECS) – c/o PO Box 60837, Nairobi, Kenya. Tel: (254-2) 56-2529. Fax: (254-2) 56-0864 or 56-1275.

Frontline Fellowship (FF) – PO Box 74, Newlands 7725, South Africa. Tel: (27-21) 689-4480. Fax: (27-21) 685-5884. E-mail: frontfel@gem.co.za.

Human Rights Watch Africa (HRWA) – 485 Fifth Avenue, New York, NY 10017-6104, USA.

Love in Action (LIA) – PO Box 3803,Halfway House 1685, South Africa. Tel/Fax: (27-11) 314-4626. E-mail: liahamm@iafrica.com.

New Sudan Council of Churches (NSCC) – PO Box 52802, Nairobi, Kenya. Tel: (254 – 2) 44-6966/44-8141. Fax: (254 – 2) 44-7015.

Norwegian People's Aid (NPA) – PO Box 39207, Nairobi, Kenya. Tel: (254 – 2) 4-4966/4-4141. Fax: (254 – 2) 44-7015.

Open Doors – PO Box 30870, Nairobi, Kenya. Fax: (254-2) 72-5222.

Presbyterian Church of Sudan (PCS) – c/o Across PO Box 21033, Nairobi, Kenya. Tel: (254 – 2) 22-0655/22069. Fax: (254 – 2) 33-9388 c/o ACROSS.

Samaritan's Purse (SP) – PO Box 76143, Nairobi, Kenya, Fax: (254-2) 43077.

Sudan Democratic Gazette – PO Box 2295, London W14 OND, UK.

Sudan Evangelical Christian Association (SECA), PO Box 220, Khartoum, Sudan. Tel: (249)-11-44-7213.

Sudan Literature Centre (SLC) – Lenana Road, Nairobi, Kenya. Tel: (254 – 2) 56-4141. Fax: (254 – 2) 72-6509.

Sudan Relief and Rehabilitation Association (SRRA) – Waumini House, Westtan Island, PO Box 39692, Nairobi, Kenya. Tel: (254 – 2) 74-0520.

Sudan Update – BM Box "CPRS", London WC1N 3XX, England. Tel/Fax: (1-422) 845-827. E-Mail: Sudanupdate 2 gn. apc. org. uk.

The New Sudan – Box 135, Trollhätten 46123, Sweden. Tel (46-520) 17230. Fax: (46-520) 16178. E-mail: dababura@hotmail. com.

SUDAN AT A GLANCE

Official Name: Republic of Sudan

Area: 2 505 813 square kilometres (967 500 sq. miles). (Twice the size of South Africa or equal to the USA east of the Mississippi River).

Population: 30 million in 140 ethnic groups (36% Arab, 31% Nilotic, 10% Eastern Sudanic, 6% Nuba). Average annual growth rate is estimated at 2,7%.

Population Density: 12 persons per km² (Urbanisation 26%).

Languages: 117 languages. Arabic is the official language in the North, English is the official language in the South. National literacy average 27%. (Full Bibles in 8 languages, New Testaments only – a further 17 languages, Gospels only – a further 12 languages).

Religions: Sudan declared an Islamic Republic in 1983, despite the 1972 Addis Abbaba Agreement. 70% Muslim with Sunnis predominating and Sufis as a powerful minority. 10% Animist/traditional religions. 20% Christians (growing at 10,9% annually). (Roman Catholics make up 12% and Protestants 8% of the total population).

Percentage of total land area under cultivation: 5%

Educational Enrolments: 50% of potential in a primary education.
22% of potential in secondary education.
3% of potential in tertiary education.

Gross National Product per capita: US$ 390 per year (1995).

Foreign Debt: US$ 18,5 Billion (221% of GNP) (1995).

Physical Infrastructure: 4 785 km of railway track, 2 000 km of paved roads, 80 000 telephones (3 telephones for every 1 000 people), Electricity generating capacity: 500 MW, Radio receivers: 258 per 1 000 people.

Sources: Africa at a Glance, African Institute of South Africa 1998, Operation World by Patrick Johnstone 1997.

BIBLIOGRAPHY

Egypt and the Sudan by *Scott Wayne and Danien Simons (Lonely Planet) 1994.*

Last Stands by *Craig Philip (Bison Group) 1994.*

Facing Genocide: The Nuba of Sudan by *Rakiya Omaar and Alex de Waal (Africa Rights) 1995.*

Fire and Sword in the Sudan by *Rudolf Slatin (Arnold) 1896.*

General Gordon by *Seton Churchill (Nisbet).*

History of the Moru Church in Sudan by *Peter Obadayo Tingwa (Sudan Literature Centre) 1992.*

Life of Gordon by *Demetrius Boulger (Fisher) 1896.*

Situation of Human Rights in the Sudan by *Gaspar Biro (UN Commission on Human Rights) 1996.*

Sudan – A Cry for Peace – *Report of Pax Christi 1994.*

Operation World by *Patrick Johnstone (Zondervan) 1997.*

The Church in Sudanese History by *Andrew Wheeler (Bishop Gwynne College) 1982.*

The Conflict and the Church in the Sudan by *Alew Damiano Bwoto (CCMW) 1994.*

The Last of the Nuba by *Leni Rieferstahl (Harvill Press) 1976.*

The Road to Khartoum – A life of General Charles Gordon by *Charles Chenevix Trench (Carol and Graf) 1978.*

The Tears of Orphans – *Amnesty International Report 1995.*

Vanishing Kingdoms by *John Tunstall (Purnell) 1966.*

About the Author

Rev. Peter Hammond is a missionary who has pioneered evangelistic outreaches in the war zones of Angola, Mozambique and Sudan. Often travelling by off road motorbike, Peter has travelled hundreds of thousands of kilometres to deliver Bibles to persecuted churches throughout Africa and Eastern Europe.

Peter has personally carried out over 100 missions behind enemy lines and conducted over 8 000 services, outreaches and meetings in 21 countries. In the course of his missionary activities, preaching the Gospel to all sides of the many conflicts, Peter has been ambushed, come under mortar fire, been stabbed, shot at, beaten by mobs, arrested and imprisoned.

Peter Hammond is the Founder and Director of *Frontline Fellowship* and the Director of *United Christian Action* (a network of 20 Bible based groups working for Reformation and praying for revival in Africa). He is an international speaker, presenting over 400 lectures or sermons each year throughout Africa and America. He is also the presenter of *the Christian Voice* radio programmes. As a writer he has authored numerous publications, in particular, he has written *"Holocaust in Rwanda"*, *"Faith Under Fire in Sudan"*, *"In the Killing Fields of Mozambique"* and *"Putting Feet to Your Faith"*. He is the editor of both *Frontline Fellowship News* and UCANEWS.

Peter is married to Lenora and they have been blessed with four children – Andrea, Daniela, Christopher and a new baby.

Other Publications by the Author

Biblical Principles for Southern Africa
Bybelse Beginsels vir Suider-Afrika
Biblical Worldview Seminar Manual
Die Christen in Oorlog
Discipleship Training Course Manual
Faith in Action
Faith Under Fire in Sudan
Fight For Life – A Pro-Life Handbook *(contributed to)*
Finding Freedom from the Pornography Plague
Great Commission Manual
Holocaust in Rwanda
Holocauste au Rwanda *(French Translation)*
In the Killing Fields of Mozambique
Putting Feet to Your Faith
Quo Vadis, South Africa
Security and Survival in Unstable Times
The Christian at War *(also translated into Spanish)*
The Christian Voice of Southern Africa *(edited)*

Audio Documentaries

– Africa's Agony: The Untold Story (60 min)
– Jihad and Slavery in Sudan (60 min)
– Revival Amidst Persecution in Sudan (60 min)

Video Documentaries

– In the Frontline: Evangelising in the War Zones (35 min)
– Under Fire in Sudan (25 min)

For an order form write to: Frontline Fellowship,
PO Box 74, Newlands 7725, Cape Town, South Africa.
Tel. (27-21) 689-4480 or Fax (27-21) 685-5884.
E-mail: frontfel@gem.co.za

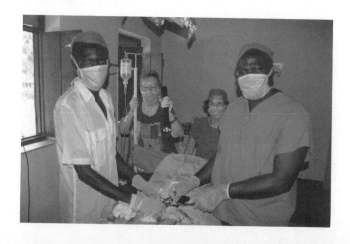